WATER RITES
IN JUDAISM

WATER RITES IN JUDAISM

As Background for Understanding Holy Ghost Baptism

CAROL E. SMITH, MTS

authorHOUSE®

AuthorHouse™
1663 Liberty Drive
Bloomington, IN 47403
www.authorhouse.com
Phone: 1 (800) 839-8640

Scripture quotations are from the HarperCollins Study Bible NRSV With the Apocryphal/ Deuterocanonical Books, Copyright 1993 by HarperCollins Publishers Inc.

Published by AuthorHouse 04/01/2015

ISBN: 978-1-5049-1111-5 (sc)
ISBN: 978-1-5049-0414-8 (e)

Library of Congress Control Number: 2015904951

CONTENTS

PREFACE

The motivation for choosing this study comes from this writer's curiosity regarding the origins of water baptism and the link between water baptism and Spirit baptism in relationship to the Church and Christianity. From the time I began studying the Bible many years ago I have been passionate about wanting to trace how religious practices and beliefs in Judaism may align with contemporary Christian practices and beliefs. The origins of Christianity are permeated in ancient Jewish religious practices and beliefs. Yet, many Christians lack information and therefore understanding about the Jewish legacy handed down to the Church. Most Christians accept that water baptism is necessary to be a part of the Christian church. They do not question who, what, when, how or why regarding the practice of water baptism.

This writer intends to furnish information and argument supporting origins of water baptism. This project is largely written for contemporary Christians but, it is hoped that it will benefit all other serious inquirers of truth as well. It is the writer's proposal to furnish background necessary to articulate a knowledgeable answer to the question, *What are the origins/roots of water baptism?* Archaic modes of ceremonial water rituals will be explored to assist Christians in understanding the underpinnings of the origins of Christian religious practices and beliefs. The scope of research includes a medley of books and articles on origins and antecedents of Christian baptism and/or initiation rites, Spirit baptism and ancient literary writing style. Books and articles used were authored by scholars in their respective fields, theology for the most part. Dictionaries and encyclopedias were consulted on water rites/ baptism and Judaism as well. The list of works consulted, though not exhaustive, covers publications authored over nearly a century which permits the author to explore scholarship on the timeless subject of origins of water rites.

The writer's purpose for this study goes forth with the hope of spurring contemporary Bible based Christians into exploring roots/origins of water baptism. The rite of water baptism (Acts 2:38) did not begin on the day of Pentecost when the Church was formulated as many Christians today believe. This is seen in churches which display markings or signs using the words, "New Testament Pattern." Water rites or baptism was a religious practice of Judaism before Christianity. Christianity has a legacy rich in Judaism.

TO

Christians Everywhere

FOREWORD

For centuries the church has struggled to understand the relationship between baptism by water and baptism by the Holy Spirit, or the Holy Ghost. Is immersion in water enough to give a person standing before God and a complete place in the Christian community (the church) as well as salvation? Can we stand before God in salvation (and have a place in the church) on the strength of the baptism of the Holy Ghost alone? Or are both necessary for complete welcome by God, participation in the life of the church, and salvation? To be a complete Christian should I receive both the water and the Spirit?

Carol Smith brings a lifetime of curiosity to this question. Some years ago she wedded this curiosity with serious study by becoming a student at Christian Theological Seminary where she completed the Master of Theological Studies degree. Everyone, of course, is free to have an opinion about such things. But Carol has gone beyond simply having an opinion to having a point of view based on serious scholarship. She has reasons and evidence for what she thinks, and she presents those things in a clear and easy-to-read way.

In addition to curiosity, Carol brought a love of the Bible with her to school. At the seminary, she applied herself to the study of the Bible as well as to the broader study of theology, always with an eye towards how these things helped her come to a deeper understanding of the Bible, Christian faith, church practice, and her own life. In 30 years of teaching at Christian Theological Seminary, I have seldom had a student with the passion for learning that exudes from Carol Smith.

I will not take away from the reader's joy of discovering how Carol answers the questions articulated above. But I need to say that she approaches these issues not only as a responsible and informed interpreter of the Bible, but also as a theologian who has the Pentecostal tradition in her bones and who writes with deep appreciation for that tradition even while seeking to enlarge its thinking at an important point. On Carol's part, this effort comes from a place of love—love for her church, love for people who can benefit from it, and most of all love for God.

Congregations and Christians in the Pentecostal movement will benefit from the way in which this book explores the deep theological and experiential significance of immersion in water (and other forms of baptism). Congregations and Christians beyond Pentecostalism who have not given as much attention to the presence and power of the

Holy Spirit will benefit from the ways in which Carol Smith highlights the importance of the Spirit as animating the Christian life. Indeed, all congregations and churches will benefit from the revelation in this book that the water and Spirit are organically connected. God works through both.

This book has been in preparation for a long time. Carol has made many trips to the library. She has turned many pages. She has pursued many trails to books and articles that are hard to find. She has stayed up too late on too many nights. In the process, she has become a clear and compelling writer.

I hope God and the church will forgive me for the weaknesses in this analogy, but it is as if Carol's time at the seminary was being plunged into the water, and the writing of this book and its publication is the outpouring of the Spirit. Of course, from Carol's point of view, the Spirit was already present in the water, in the work she did at the seminary, and the book is a kind of ongoing embodiment of having been in the water. The one led to the other, and the other confirmed the one. Carol is that kind of biblical interpreter, writer, and Christian: the complete package.

Ronald J. Allen
Professor of Preaching and Gospels and Letters
Christian Theological Seminary

INTRODUCTION

Contemporary Christian denominations use some version of the Bible to develop doctrine in the study of theology. Hermeneutics, however, differ. Many Christians see the contemporary church patterned after the first century church instituted in Jerusalem. Judaism provided the antecedents of many Christian religious practices and beliefs. Indeed some Christian practices and beliefs were adopted from Judaism by the Church. One such practice is the ritual of water baptism. Herein I will examine the practice of water baptism as well as Spirit baptism. Baptism is administered through the use of certain ceremonial water rituals such as affusion, immersion, submersion and aspersion.

I will primarily focus on the origins of water rites in Judaism and compare water baptism in Luke-Acts to Jewish water rites prior to the Jesus movement. Chapter One will explore general ancient water rites of various peoples including water rites in Judaism prior to the Jesus movement. What are the origins/roots of water baptism? This author believes that for contemporary Christianity simply to accept water baptism as part of the indoctrination process into the Christian religious tradition without knowing its origins or roots is baseless. It impedes one's ability to explore the possibility that water baptism is a religious practice passed on to Christianity from Judaism religious practices; that a linkage between water baptism and Spirit baptism may exist.

Before beginning to examine practices of water baptism introduced in Luke-Acts in Chapter Two, I will establish that water baptism as a Jewish religious practice was in place when the Church started. Chapter Three will investigate water baptism and Spirit baptism in Luke-Acts in comparison to and in relationship to Jewish water rites. It is this writer's understanding based on the genre of Luke-Acts, that the writer purposefully molded the narrative to persuade audiences to assume the author's own theological views. Careful rhetorical construction of documents was in vogue during the time of the writing of Luke-Acts.[1] Scholars today agree that Luke-Acts does not merely report facts rather they agree that Luke-Acts posits Luke's own story of Jesus and the early church.

Aune describes the writer of Luke-Acts as a Hellenistic historian possessing Greek rhetoric credentials in a Greco-Roman world.

---

[1] David E. Aune, *The New Testament in Its Literary Environment*, ed. Wayne Meeks (Philadelphia: The Westminister Press, 1987) 77.

According to Aune Luke should not be separated from Acts, the two belong together.[2] Allen, author of "The Story of Jesus According to 'Luke' – The Gospel of Luke," characterizes Luke as a "remarkable storyteller."[3] Allen further points out how "Luke creates a narrative world organized by a journey motif." [4] While Luke's listeners envision the trajectory of Jesus and the early church, Luke is able to sway listeners theologically.[5] On the other hand, Bloomberg points to a consensus of scholars who see Luke's theology in certain places, as inherently Mosaic.[6] I will show that the writer of Luke-Acts has general background knowledge of the ritual of water rites in Judaism. I am interested in how the writer makes use of echoes of Jewish water rites in first century writings of Luke-Acts and how this may line up with the Christian Church's water baptism rite today.

Few in Western contemporary Christian churches understand or consider origins of water baptism though most adhere to some sort of doctrinal guidance regarding water baptism as well as Spirit baptism. For instance, the exegetical setting in the Apostolic Pentecostal Church excludes anyone who does not follow a specific formula for being "born

---

[2]   Ibid.

[3]   Ronald J. Allen, "The Story of Jesus According to 'Luke' The Gospel of Luke" in *Chalice Introduction to the New Testament,* ed. Dennis Smith (St. Louis: Chalice Press, 2004), 176.

[4]   Ibid., 185.

[5]   Ibid.

[6]   Craig L. Blomberg, "The Law In Luke-Acts," *Journal for the Study of the New Testament* 22 (1984): 53-80.

again" or saved according to the formula in Acts 2:38. The teaching regarding Spiritual rebirth includes water baptism by immersion and receiving the Holy Spirit. Baptism is accomplished when a candidate for baptism walks down the steps into a pool of water. The water covers some of the steps and the candidate stands in water about waist-high. In a way, the steps remind me of a miqveh which had steps descending down into a pool of water.[7] As the person stands in the water, a minister repeats Acts 2:38 (paraphrasing) while supporting the baptismal candidate's back and dunks the person underwater bringing him/her back up into a standing position.

In order to be saved or "born again" the Apostolic Church teaches that the following formula is mandatory: (1) repentance, (2) water baptism by immersion in Jesus' Name, and (3) Holy Ghost baptism which is supported with evidence of speaking in tongues (Acts 2). Only persons who conform to this formula are considered to be saved or born again in the Apostolic Pentecostal faith church assembly. Though I supported this process in the past I believe that only God can judge whether or not a person is saved. I do not believe that persons in other Christian denominations and religious traditions are not saved if they do not conform to the formula carried out in the Apostolic Pentecostal

---

[7]   William Sanford La Sor, "Discovering What Jewish Miqva'ot Can Tell Us About Christian Baptism," *Biblical Archaeology Review* 1 (January/February 1987): 52-59.

faith. I say this because there is only one God, and God, not any human being, is the final judge.

Furthermore, my interpretation of Acts 2 has changed since becoming aware of the fact that my home church is an exclusive institution. My understanding of an exclusive church is garnered from Eck's explanation of the exclusivist response: "Our own community, our tradition, our understanding of reality, our encounter with God, is the one and only truth excluding all others."[8] My home church is steeped in tradition under the leadership of the Pentecostal Assemblies of the World, Inc. who declare: ". . . no person is to be given the right hand of fellowship as a member in our church unless he is baptized in water in Jesus' Name and filled with the Holy Spirit (Ghost) with Biblical evidence of speaking in other Tongues as the Spirit of God giveth utterance."[9]

I no longer support an exclusive Christian religious view of the Church. I do however fully support Christianity and I believe I am saved through the redemptive work of Jesus Christ. I am interested in re-evaluating the exclusive view of Apostolic Pentecostalism and looking deeper into the subject of pluralism beginning with Eck's approach. Eck's pluralist response states, ". . . we recognize the limits of the world

---

[8] Diana L. Eck, *Encountering God: A Spiritual Journey from Bozeman to Banaras* (Boston: Beacon Press, 1993), 168.

[9] Organization Manual *2004 Minute Book* (Indianapolis: Pentecostal Assemblies of the World, Inc. 2005), 117.

we already know and we seek to understand others in their own terms, not just in ours."[10]

At one time I interpreted the Bible in the same manner as that taught in my home church congregation. However, I have come to interpret some parts of the Bible differently. Since I was introduced to the subject of pluralism in the Master of Theological Studies 2005 Colloquium Class (X 820) at Christian Theological Seminary I have come to support a somewhat different view of religious traditions. I no longer believe in an exclusive Church. I believe in the Church of Jesus Christ recorded in the Bible (Matt. 16:18).

---

[10] Diana L Eck, *Encountering God: A Spiritual Journey from Bozeman to Banaras.* 169.

CHAPTER ONE

Ancient Water Rites in Various Cultures

As a young child I can recall hearing mythical stories involving some watery milieu, the legend of Jonah in the belly of a large whale—Jonah prayed and the whale spit Jonah out onto dry land, the story of Noah and the ark—all who entered into the ark would be saved from a flood that would wipe out all civilization on earth, Moses and the Hebrew people crossing the Red Sea—they were delivered or saved from Pharaoh and, Jesus being baptized by John in the Jordan River while a dove descended over Jesus. The mythic dimension of these stories has been repeated for generations, including by great storytellers like my parents and grandparents.[11] The Jonah, Noah, Moses and Jesus myths

---

[11] Accounts of Jonah, Noah, Moses and Jesus are recorded in the Hebrew Bible; however, it should be noted that I first heard these stories before I personally

1

serve only to provide a means to explicate that myths and/or legends about water are numerous and have existed throughout the ages.

In this chapter I begin by surveying how water functioned as a symbol in primeval water myths. I will then focus on water rites in the Hebrew Bible and conclude by exploring how and why water rites were executed in the communities of the Essenes and the Pharisees prior to the Jesus movement. As I explore water myths of various peoples I find it useful to call attention to Eliade's explanation of myth functions and rituals. The main function of a myth Eliade asserts is "to determine the exemplar models of all ritual, and of all significant human acts."[12]

Primeval Water Myths, Legends and Symbolization

Water myths and beliefs have long been embraced by various peoples dating back to primeval times. Water symbolization is very much a part of creation myths. The Torah tells of creation beginning when God created the heavens and earth; earth was a formless void and darkness was upon the waters and God spoke light into existence. God spoke all creation into existence and gave order to chaos in creation: "Let the waters under the sky be gathered together into one place. . ." and "God called the . . . waters that were gathered together . . . Seas."

---

learned of them in the Bible. They were traditions passed down to me by my parents and grandparents.

[12] Mircea Eliade, *Patterns in Comparative Religion* (New York: Sheed & Ward, 1958), 410

(Gen. 1:9-10)[13] Polynesian creation myth too tells of a void with the existence only of primordial waters, cosmic darkness when Io, the supreme god, awakened and light appeared and the heavens were formed. Io spoke the world into existence.[14] Water, Eliade explains ". . . is *fons et origo,* the source of all possible existence."[15] Eliade's theory on water captures the essence of water in creation:

> In cosmogony, in myth, ritual and iconography, water fills the same function in whatever type of cultural pattern we find it; it *precedes* all forms and *upholds* all creation. Immersion in water symbolizes a return to the pre-formal, a total regeneration, a new birth, for immersion means a dissolution of forms, a reintegration into the formlessness of pre-existence; and emerging from the water is a repetition of the act of creation in which form was first expressed. Every contact with water implies regeneration: first, because dissolution is succeeded by a "new birth", and then because immersion fertilizes, increases the potential of life and of creation. In initiation rituals, water confers a "new birth", in

---

13 The HarperCollins Study Bible NRSV With the Apocryphal/Deuterocanonical Books will be used to quote all Bible References throughout this thesis.

14 Mircea Eliade, *Patterns in Comparative Religion* (New York: Sheed & Ward, 1958), 410

15 Ibid., 188.

magic rituals it heals, and in funeral rites it assures rebirth after death. Because it incorporates in itself all potentiality, water becomes a symbol of life ("living water").[16]

Considering this statement, we can deduce that water symbolization embodies an overall connection in creation.

Dating back to prehistoric times civilizations have used hieroglyphs for water patterns or images to portray beliefs. Rites involving water use were often seen in non-Jewish pagan religions. Other myths and legends told of ancient creation beliefs involving water include the Babylonian creation legend that speaks of a watery chaos.[17] Since primitive times myths believed by various peoples have conceived water as an element linked with the moon and a woman as the path of fertility for man and the universe. Eliade asserts, "At every level of existence, water is a source of life."[18] Of fertilization Eliade states, "Water nourishes life, rain fertilizes as does the *semen virile*. In the erotic symbolism of the creation, the sky embraces and fertilizes the earth with rain. This same symbolism is found universally."[19] Further expounding on water symbolization

---

[16]   Ibid.
[17]   Ibid., 191.
[18]   Ibid., 190.
[19]   Ibid., 192.

Eliade states, "In initiation rituals, water confers a "new birth. . ."" and "immersion in water symbolizes . . . a total regeneration ."[20]

Mesopotamians, Wakuta and Trobriand Islanders, Pima Indians all believed some mythical tradition connected to water. Water has been referred to as Mother Earth, Living Water; it has served as a medicinal component. Even today, the phrase "fountain of youth" is used universally. Eliade asserts, "Karaja Indians in Brazil recall a mythological time when 'they still lived in the water."[21] Another mythical water ritual includes newborn babies in Mexico being consecrated to the goddess of waters, Chalchihuitlycue Chalchiuhtlatonac. This was part of a baptismal washing ritual that involved being immersed in water. The baptismal washing is symbolic of cleansing newborn babes of the sins and imperfections passed on to them by their parents.[22] In the Hebrew Bible the deluge presents an example of water as a symbol of deliverance.

Since the rise of civilization in the ancient Near East water has been used for its purifying properties. Primeval water myths, legends and symbols practiced by various peoples and/or cultures are mentioned here as examples that serve as precursors to the focus of this thesis,

---

[20]   Ibid., 188-89

[21]   Ibid., 191

[22]   Ibid., 192. Chalchihuitlycue, goddess of water, was looked on as the real mother of the newborn babies. This is similar to Christian beliefs that view God as our real Father. The rite of baptismal washing through immersion in water in the Christian Church symbolizes cleansing from sin passed on to mankind from Adam and Eve.

water rites in Judaism as background for Spirit baptism in Luke-Acts. Myriad religious traditions used ceremonial water rites in ancient times including the Jews.

Water Rites in Judaism Prior to the Jesus Movement

Moving along towards the crux of this writing I will now discuss water rights in Judaism notably prior to the Jesus Movement. During the tribal confederacy period of Hebrew/Jewish civilization around 1250 B.C.E., the priests were required by commandment of God punishable by death, to use the water in the laver to wash their hands and feet before entering the Tabernacle in the wilderness at Sinai (Exodus 30).[23] So we find that the Hebrew/Jewish people have adhered to an elaborate system of water purification rituals long before the Common Era. Purification lustration ceremonies have been performed using water for healing and cleansing in a religious and physical sense since primitive times. The Hebrew Bible records God giving Moses instructions on the techniques of purification rites when a person suffered a disease or physical impurity.

A person suffering from the disease of leprosy, for instance, was required to undergo a mandatory intricate purification cleansing ritual. During one fraction of the purification process the leper was required to bathe his body in water and wash his clothes. Purification rites were

---

[23]   Russell Peagnant, *Engaging the New Testament: An Interdisciplinary Introduction* (Minneapolis: Fortress Press, 1995), 52

administered by a priest (Leviticus chapter 14). The Torah is saturated with accounts of God's commandments to Hebrew peoples regarding water purification rituals (e.g., Ex. 40:12, 30-32; Lev. 8:6; 16:4, 24). On water purification rituals Hyatt explains,

> In the Old Testament we find some purification rites in pre-exilic times, but it is likely that these were multiplied and emphasized in post-exilic times. Most of the purification rites that we know in detail are described in the Priestly Code. With the rise of Pharisaic Judaism in the first and second centuries B.C., increasing emphasis was placed on these, since the Pharisees believed that many of the rules for priests should be applied to laymen also.

> Various objects or actions might cause a person to be unclean or impure, and often one of the things prescribed for purification was the use of water, by washing, immersion or sprinkling.[24]

Purification rites using water flourished in Judaism centuries before the time of Jesus and John the Immerser.

---

[24] Philip J. Hyatt, "The Origin and Meaning of Christian Baptism." *Encounter* 21:1 (Winter 1960): 255-268.

In Jewish tradition some actions that might deem persons unclean include touching an animal that died of itself or was torn by wild animals (Lev. 17:15-16), a man with semen discharge and a woman menstruating (Lev.15:13-32).[25] Deuteronomy Chapter 23 addresses purity in the camp: anyone in the (military) camp who became unclean due to nocturnal emission was to go to an area outside the camp. At evening time the unclean person was to wash himself with water and when the sun had set he could return to the camp. Before Jews could enter the Temple, they were required to immerse themselves in what is termed, "living water" in order to become ritually clean. "Living water" is considered running water like that in a stream or river.[26]

This rite was carried on both upon visits to the Temple and when the Temple no longer existed. "Living" water explains Ricks is flowing water. Miqveh ritual immersions took place in "living water."[27] Eliade says that water incorporates all potentiality within itself thus becoming a symbol of life or living water. From this perspective I see living water as nurturing one's entire being. Another lustration that was carried out in ancient Judaism was proselyte baptism which allowed non-Jews to convert to Judaism.

---

[25] Ibid. Hyatt points out that since 1948 there has been a renewed interest in the ritual of baptism. This observation would be about a decade after Hyatt's 1960 *Encounter* article. The Dead Sea Scrolls would have brought about this renewed interest in the rite and origin of baptism.

[26] Ibid.

[27] Stephen D. Ricks, "Miqvaot: Ritual Immersion Baths in Second Temple (Intertestamental) Jewish History." *BYU Studies* 36:3 (1996-1997): 277-286.

There has been much debate on when proselyte baptism commenced. However, as the following authors suggest, there is ample reason to think that some in Judaism did practice these rites prior to the Jesus movement. Gilmore and Zeitlin are two scholars who feel proselyte baptism commenced in first century, others however think it began in the second century.[28] Zeitlin explains that it is the opinion of nearly all New Testament Scholars that proselyte baptism among the Jews was in vogue long before Jesus.[29] While Zeitlin further asserts proselyte baptism was practiced in the first century, it was the latter part of the first century, ca. 65 C.E., rather than before or during the time of Jesus. He makes an intense argument as to when proselyte baptism commenced.

After a full investigation of the origin of proselyte baptism and a historic investigation of the Talmud on this subject, Zeitlin claims that Jews did not adopt proselyte baptism until just before the destruction of the second Temple. He does however suggest that early Christians adopted proselyte baptism from the Jews.[30] While Zeitlin and others acknowledge that proselyte baptism was not adopted by the Jews until just before the destruction of the second Temple, I find it difficult

---

[28] A. Gilmore, "Jewish Antecedents," in *Christian Baptism: A Fresh Attempt to Understand the Rite in Terms of Scripture, History and Theology,* ed. A. Gilmore, intro. E.A. Payne. (Chicago: Judson Press, 1959), 67.

[29] Solomon Zeitlin, "The Halaka In the Gospels and its Relation to the Jewish Law at the Time of Jesus." *Hebrew Union College Annual* 1.01 (2006): 357-373.

[30] Ibid.

to see how they continue to hold firm to their hypothesis since the Qumran and Masada archeological discoveries identify what appear to be immersion baths used for baptism and other purification rites. As this writer sees it these discoveries would be sufficient to re-evaluate claims that proselyte baptism was adopted by the Jews in late first century.

In addition there is a question that lingers in my mind regarding using the Talmud to pinpoint ancient dates: With the redaction of the Mishnah ca. 200 C.E., how can we be certain of specific dates and/or happenings such as the period just prior to the destruction of the second Temple, prior to the time of reconstruction. Allen and Williamson state that "We do not know that the sayings from Jewish sources go back to the time of Jesus or before."[31] On the other hand though, these scholars explain ". . . it is the case that sayings from an oral tradition obviously antedate their being written and preserved in documents."

Based on this writer's examination on the subject of proselyte baptism, I join the majority of New Testament scholars who suggest that proselyte baptism was practiced prior to Jesus. This writer also sides with the following authors. Gavin suggests that proselyte baptism would have been a natural practice in Judaism considering the frequency of immersion baths in any number of purification instances stipulated

---

[31] Ronald J. Allen and Clark M. Williamson, *Preaching the Gospels without Blaming the Jews: A Lectionary Commentary* (Louisville: Westminster John Knox Press, 2004), xxiv-xxv.

under the Law. Pusey and Hunt claim that "Evidence for proselyte baptism within the Rabbinic sources is of uncertain date." [32] Gilmore and Zeitlin both claim a specific timeline. On the other hand Hyatt argues,

> For our purpose, the question regarding the date of origin of Jewish proselyte baptism is important. Most of our information concerning it comes from the Talmud, and other relatively late sources. However, there are indications that the rite was practiced before the destruction of the temple in 70 A.D., and that it originated before the time of John and Jesus. [33]

Hyatt argues that his research information comes from later sources yet he embraces the notion that proselyte baptism originated before the time of John and Jesus.

Gavin states that from 150 B.C. to 66 C.E. severe Jewish legislation dealing with Gentile susceptibility of impurity was enacted. [34] He further

---

[32] Karen Pusey and John Hunt. "Jewish Proselyte Baptism." *The Expository Times* 95:1 (October 1983): 141-145.

[33] Hyatt, "The Origin and Meaning of Christian Baptism." 255-268. Much of the information on the subject of Jewish proselyte baptism comes from the Mishnah. This Rabbinic source was written ca. 200 C.E., much later than the events covered; thus it is uncertain when proselyte baptism commenced.

[34] F. Gavin, *Jewish Antecedents of the Christian Sacraments.* (London: Society for Promoting Christian Knowledge, 1928), vi.

affirms that one part of a convert's admission to Judaism was comprised of a ceremonial self-immersion—the *tebilah*, or baptism prior to the Christian era; that this practice followed instructions in the Priest's Code.[35] Gavin explains,

> From the first century on, references to Proselyte Baptism are numerous. That it could be a matter of debate by the end of the first century suggests definitely that it had been a long prevailing practice, and the incident alluded to in Pes. VIII. 8 reinforces the inference of proscriptive use of a much earlier date. When the authorities of the Talmud have to deal with this Mishna their recorded opinions show how the clue to the origin and significance of the rite lay outside their ken.

> The Baptism of Proselytes would be an obvious and natural procedure. The Law prescribed an immersion-bath for purification in a dozen instances.[36]

It seems then, that at some time during second or first century B.C.E. proselyte baptism commenced. The exact date of commencement

---

[35]   Ibid., vii.

[36]   Ibid., 31. Pes. VIII. 8 refers to Mishna Pesahim VIII. 8.

however is unknown. Proselyte baptism is just one of many water rites explored herein. I will continue by discussing other water rites practiced by subgroups in Judaism, the Essenes and Pharisees.

Water Rites of the Qumran Essenes

It is important to elucidate the Jewish setting around the first century in order to capture the environment in which Jews lived and carried out their religious beliefs and practices. Under the rule of Julius Caesar (ca. 46-44 C.E.) the *magna carta* of the Jews in the Roman Empire was formed. This allowed the Jews to live according to their religious traditions. Thus, for the most part, the Jews were allowed to rule within their own law and follow their customs and observances. Allen and Williamson explain the situation of Jews living in the Roman Empire thusly: "They were in captivity in their own land, in exile at home, under occupation by a series of emperors who claimed to be God."[37] Although Jews as well as other religious traditions were permitted to practice their religions, different strands of Judaism existed including the Essenes and the Pharisees. Each sect differed expressing their own religious beliefs and/or practices.

The Qumran Essenes were a Jewish community that had broken away from the Temple Jews. Josephus, a Pro-Roman Jewish historian,

---

[37] Ronald J. Allen and Clark M. Williamson, *Preaching the Gospels without Blaming The Jews: A Lectionary Commentary.* xix.

who lived around the same time as Luke and the Essenes, characterizes Qumran as a Jewish community living in self-imposed segregation in eschatological anticipation of the coming of the Lord.[38] The first century writings of Josephus and discovery of the Dead Sea Scrolls in 1947 support belief that Jewish water rituals included customary practices of washings, immersions and ritual baths. Most scholars recognize Qumran as the site where the Essenes resided. The 1947 Dead Sea Scrolls (Qumran Scrolls) document the existence of physical remains such as baptismal pools, cisterns and water supply systems in first and second century B.C.E.

In addition to many scholars believing the Essenes resided at Qumran, some surmise that John the Immerser lived near the same general region and he may have been connected with the Essenes. Regarding any association between the Essenes and John, Hyatt asserts that this is "made much more probable by the new discoveries at Qumran. Both John and the Qumran Essenes had a strong eschatological emphasis."[39] Various water rites were common in the Qumran community.

---

[38] Maxwell Johnson, *The Rites of Christian Initiation: Their Evolution and Interpretation* (Collegeville: The Liturgical Press, 1999), 7. Here Johnson points out that there are several theories on the subject of the origination of John's baptism. Some scholars theorize that John's baptism comes from John's own method of baptism which echoed that of the Essene community at Qumran near the Dead Sea or from the initiation ritual of proselyte baptism required of all Gentiles converts to Judaism.

[39] Hyatt, "The Origin and Meaning of Christian Baptism." 255-268.

Nearly sixty years have passed since 800 different manuscripts were discovered at Qumran. Legend tells of how "a young bedouin shepherd . . . accidentally discovered in an inaccessible cave next to Wadi Qumran, on the shores of the Dead Sea, a set of ancient Hebrew and Aramaic manuscripts deposited in the bottom of some jars."[40] Commenting on these manuscripts Martinez says,

> These manuscripts encompass the whole of the Hebrew Bible and the wide field of apocryphal writings (to which they add a large number of previously unknown works). Also, a great quantity of writings which reveal to us the organization, beliefs and religious aspirations of the ancient Jewish sect from whose library all these manuscripts come and whose centre has been discovered close to the caves.

> One of the most sensational elements from this discovery was the antiquity of these texts. All the manuscripts are earlier than the catastrophe of 70 C.E. and a large part comes from the 1st and 2nd centuries BCE.[41]

---

[40] Florentino Garcia Martinez, "The Dead Sea Scrolls, Jesus Christ and Origins of Christianity" in *The People of the Dead Sea Scrolls*, trans. Wilfred G.E. Watson (Leiden: Brill, 1995), 193.

[41] Ibid.

Discovery of the Qumran texts, both sectarian and intertestamental, casts new light on the period in which Christianity was formed and rabbinic Judaism was shaped. Upon discovery, these texts were free of Jewish and Christian censorship. The ancient writings of the texts prove they were composed between the third century B.C.E. and the middle of the first century C.E.[42] These findings also define Qumran community practices, beliefs and traditions during this period.

The Qumran discoveries document the existence of physical remains (i.e., water pools, cisterns, water supply system) in first and second century B.C.E. Hyatt asserts that the Dead Sea Scrolls or Qumran Scrolls and the excavations at Khirbet Qumran show that from second century B.C.E. to 70 C.E., a community existed in which lustrations were essential; that in the community center where the excavations took place several pools or cisterns were found and that there can be no doubt that some were used for ritualistic purposes.[43] Signs of worn steps leading down into the water can be seen in one of the larger pools. The seven cisterns discovered at Qumran were linked by an overpass or bridge that supplied water to them and they may have been used for ritual washings or baptismal rites.[44] Drawing from archaeologist

---

[42]   Ibid., 197.

[43]   Hyatt, "The Origin and Meaning of Christian Baptism." 255-268.

[44]   John Pryke, "The Sacraments of Holy Baptism and Holy Communion In the Light of The Ritual Washings and Sacred Meals at Qumran." *Revue De Qumran* 17 (October 1964): 543-552.

findings in the early seventies Ricks states, "The water installations at Qumran have recently been persuasively shown to be miqvaot."[45]

Could these pools have been used for proselyte baptism? Were they not used for all types of ceremonial lustrations (e.g., washings, immersions and ritual baths)? Design and construction of the pools could readily facilitate baptism by immersion in water (e.g., proselyte baptism). The Qumran Essenes were also known as Hemerobaptists as some began each day with a ritual bath to insure that they were free from the possibility of defilement.

In the early sixties excavations of the residence of King Herod the Great (ca. 37- 4 C.E.) in Masada also uncovered miqveh installations. Also in the seventies near the Dung Gate outside the Old City of Jerusalem, an archeologist discovered several miqva'ot in the homes of wealthy families. Ricks uses Wood's work to point out that the Qumran community had twice the water they needed to maintain themselves and suggests that the excess water was used for ritual baths.[46] Using the same study (Wood's) La Sor states, "A recent (1984) study . . . has shown rather conclusively that some of the water installations at Qumran were indeed miqva'ot."[47]

---

[45] Stephen D. Ricks, "Miqvaot: Ritual Immersion Baths in Second Temple (Intertestamental) Jewish History." 277-286.

[46] Ibid.

[47] La Sor, "Discovering What Jewish Miqva'ot Can Tell Us About Christian Baptism." 52-59.

Pryke asserts that the Essenes' prerequisite for becoming a part of the community included a waiting period and three ritual washings; that the bath was not isolated but was part of the communal way of life regarding purity.[48] It is unknown how long the first stage lasted but the second and third stages lasted a year. The Essenes' commitment to purity was such that they had broken off from the Temple as they regarded the Temple priests (Zadokite priesthood) as illegitimate and non-adherent to Essene standards of purity. Ritual washings in the Essene community were no doubt also taken before each meal in likeness to the Pharisees suggests Pryke.[49]

Qumran community zealots held an apocalyptic view and thus segregated themselves from other Jewish sects and waited on the "Day of the Lord." They spent their time preparing and purifying themselves as they waited on God to return and restore the present evil day to a new age. Since they no longer offered sacrifices in the Temple Pryke suggests that they made and offered there own (pure and worthy) sacrifices at Qumran until such time as their own priests would be able to offer worthy sacrifices in the Jerusalem Temple.[50] Their purification practices were associated with being prepared and ready for the apocalypse.

---

[48] Pryke, "The Sacraments of Holy Baptism and Holy communion In the Light of The Ritual Washings and Sacred Meals at Qumran." 543-552.

[49] Ibid.

[50] Ibid.

Water Rites of the Pharisees

Previously in this chapter I explored how purification water rituals were practiced in the ancient Near East and water symbolism linked thereto. Now, water rites practiced by another lay renewal movement in Judaism, the Pharisees, will be mentioned briefly for the purpose of further illustrating Jewish water purification practices prior to the Jesus movement. Scholars identify the Pharisees as a somewhat small Judaic group, about six thousand strong.[51] Ancient purity laws permeated a major part of their lifestyle. Most notably, this sect observed the laws of ritual purity outside the Temple where everyone else kept them.

Pharisaic Jews carried over the practice of immersion in "living water" required before entering the Temple into their homes. For the Pharisees ritual purity was compulsory for all meals eaten at home. Their table-fellowship depended solely on observance of the Torah. Keeping the Pharisaic rule required "perpetual sanctification of daily life through rite"[52] Neusner explains: "The laws of cultic contamination . . . extended even to objects upon which unclean

---

[51]   Jacob Neusner, *Judaism in the Beginning of Christianity* (Philadelphia: Fortress Press, 1984), 45.
      The Pharisees had a strict adherence to the Torah and oral traditional teachings. Ritual purity was of paramount concern especially regarding meals in which case ritual washings no doubt preceded the sacred meal.

[52]   Ibid., 58.

persons (such as are listed in Leviticus 15) stood, sat, or lay."[53] The Bible states:

> When any man has a discharge from his member, his discharge makes him ceremonially unclean. . . . Every bed on which the one with the discharge lies shall be unclean . . . and everything on which he sits shall be unclean. Anyone who touches his bed shall wash his clothes, and bathe in water . . . All who sit on anything on which the one with the discharge has sat shall wash their clothes, and bathe in water . . . All who touch the body of the one with the discharge shall wash their clothes, and bathe in water (Lev. 15:2-7)

And so, we find that the Torah stipulates requirements using water rites for purification purposes. The Pharisees practiced baptismal ablutions which included a rite of initiation into the sect by immersion of the entire family in water.[54]

Thus far in this chapter I have established that water rites existed and were employed in cultural and religious practices in the ancient Near East prior to the Jesus movement. Moving ahead I will investigate

---

[53] Ibid., 60.

[54] Thomas F. Torrance, The Origins of Baptism, *Scottish Journal of Theology* 11 (1958): 158-171.

how water rites in Judaism changed early in the first century C.E. Existence of and patterns in various Judaism lustrations including purification rites described in the Priestly Code, proselyte baptism, immersion-baths, immersion in living water, washings of the body and cloths, have been formulated. I will now proceed to look at how these water rites may interweave or compare to water baptism and Spirit baptism rites in Luke-Acts.

CHAPTER TWO

Holy Ghost Baptism in Comparison to Jewish Water Rites

This chapter will show how ancient water rites in Judaism prior to the Jesus movement compare to water baptism in Luke-Acts or Holy Ghost baptism commencing with the inauguration of Jesus' formal ministry in the first century, ca. 30 C.E. Johnson explains that ". . . Jesus submitted himself at the beginning of his public ministry and it is this event which provided the foundation and paradigm for the development of specifically Christian practices of baptismal initiation."[55] I will primarily devote this segment of my writing to how Luke makes

---

[55]   Maxwell Johnson, *The Rites of Christian Initiation: Their Evolution and Interpretation.* 7.

use of echoes of Jewish water rites as background for understanding Holy Ghost or Holy Spirit baptism set forth in Luke-Acts.

I will examine Luke-Acts as one book rather than separating them out. I will largely seek out and analyze key New Testament texts specific to baptism in Luke-Acts but, I will use other Scriptural texts suitable for support of my thesis discussion. The key texts are: Luke 3:3-18; Acts 1:4-8, 2:1-4, 37-39, 10:44-47, 11:14-16, 8:35-39 and 19:1-6. I will identify connections and contrasts in water baptism and Spirit baptism as I determine that ancient water rites in Judaism underpin baptism in Luke-Acts.

Luke 3:3-18
John's Water Baptism

At the outset of the gospel Luke presents two prominent characters, Jesus and John. He foretells of their births and sets the platform for tracking these two historical and prophetic (God-sent) characters. Also, a historical timeline is established—the fifteenth year of the reign of the Emperor Tiberius, Pontius Pilate, Governor of Judea, Herod, ruler of Galilee and so forth (Luke chapter 1). Luke's story continues with John's proclamation of baptism of repentance for the forgiveness of sins. John's baptism holds all Jews accountable for repentance and calls for a new (water) baptism rite for forgiveness of sins in anticipation of the coming of the Messiah. This water rite is a divergence from Old Testament instances of religious washings.

Luke presents a particular interpretation of John's water rites. Luke portrays John as a prophet endowed with the word of God stating, "the word of God came to John son of Zechariah in the wilderness." (Lu 3:2) Prior to that Luke shows Zachariah being filled with the Holy Spirit and speaking prophecy concerning his son, "And you, child, will be called the prophet of the Most High; for you will go before the Lord to prepare his ways, to give knowledge of salvation to his people by the forgiveness of their sins." (Lu 1:76-77). John fulfilled this prophecy and "went into all the region around the Jordan, proclaiming a baptism of repentance for the forgiveness of sins, as it is written in the book of the words of the prophet Isaiah" (Lu 3:2-4)

John, like the Qumran community likely did not adhere to Temple worship. It appears that there is little doubt that John's baptismal practices actually took place based on several written sources on the subject as follows: the four New Testament Gospels, the Gospel of the Ebionites, the Gospel according to the Hebrews, writings of Ignatius of Antioch and Justin Martyr.[56] But, it is uncertain when John's baptism commenced. From where did John's baptismal ritual begin? Some scholars tend to see it as having derived from the Essenes at Qumran or

---

[56]   Kenan B. Osborne, *The Christian Sacraments of Initiation: Baptism, Confirmation, Eucharist* (New York: Paulist Press, 1987), 30.

from proselyte baptism of non-Jews converting to Judaism.[57] To Luke the inception of John's baptism is not the priority. The urgency in Luke's story telling is that John's posture concerning baptism of repentance exemplifies a profound apocalyptic eschatological orientation. Thus, it is certainly highly plausible that John's baptismal rite is derived from the Essenes at Qumran. If not, John and the Qumran community share the same apocalyptic orientation. For John the end time is imminently at hand.[58] Regarding baptism Smith asserts,

> John took over this practice from the Essenes at Qumran, but he also modified it. He performed the washing in water for the forgiveness of sins as an eschatological act and, in addition, ascribed to the Messiah the eschatological cleansing with the Spirit. Thus, the Essene practices at Qumran do form the background of John's baptism as John appropriated the rite, creatively modified it, and included within his purview a role for the Coming One.[59]

---

[57] Maxwell Johnson, *The Rites of Christian Initiation: Their Evolution and Interpretation*, 7.

[58] Derwood Smith, "Jewish Proselyte Baptism and the Baptism of John." *Restoration Quarterly* 25:1 (first quarter 1982): 13-29.

[59] Ibid.

Luke is intent on inducing audience acceptance of John, the prophet, who came as a forerunner to Jesus, the prophet, on a mission to announce the advent of the Messiah. Scripture text from the Hebrew Bible, Isaiah 40:3, is a reference point used as Luke moves towards the pivotal point, salvation and Jesus as God's agent of salvation. Luke-Acts is decisively engineered so as to create a milieu that will set the stage for Jesus and His saving work for Jews and Gentiles. John arrived on the scene proclaiming an apocalyptic call to repentance with a similar yet different type baptism.

John's water baptism technique was parallel to that seen in Pharisaic Jewish immersions. Although the Priestly Code described purification rites the rise of Pharisaic Judaism in first and second centuries B.C. placed a deeper emphasis thereon.[60] But, with John's baptism the focus (departure from common purification practices) and the location were different. Lathrop says,

> By a kind of prophetic sign then, John indicates and anticipates God's coming to wash the people. Both the location and the practice of having people be baptized point to the imminence and centrality of God's action

---

[60] Hyatt, "The Origin and Meaning of Christian Baptism." 255-268. Hyatt claims that with the growth of purification practices in later times the Mishnah, Yoma iii 5 supports a ruling that no one is to perform Temple service in the Temple Court without immersion even though he is clean. Also, the High priest was to immerse himself five times on the Day of Atonement.

rather than private human action for the sake of ritual purity.[61]

Regardless of where the baptismal rites of the historical John originated, Luke echoes Jewish water rites in his presentation of John's baptism.

According to Luke, John sounded the alarm for Jews and Gentiles introducing a one-time (water) baptism of repentance for the forgiveness of sins while heralding the good news that someone greater than he was coming with a baptism of the Holy Spirit and fire (Lu 3:16).[62] Luke explains that John taught the crowds who came to partake of this (new) ritual of water baptism of repentance. John replied when "Soldiers also asked him, 'And we, what should we do?' He said to them, 'Do not extort money from anyone by threats or false accusation, and be satisfied your wages." (Luke 3:14)[63]

In the gospel of Luke, John's preaching is designed to warn people to prepare for the apocalypse. Baptism is the definitive sign of preparation for it signifies that they have repented of their sins and are

---

[61] Gordon W. Lathrop, "Baptism in the New Testament and its Cultural Settings" in *Worship and Culture in Dialogue*, ed. S. Anita Stauffer (Switzerland: Lutheran World Federation, 1994) 31.

[62] Hyatt, "The Origin and Meaning of Christian Baptism." 255-268. Hyatt says that John baptized those who were already Jews and maybe some (Gentile) Roman soldiers.

[63] The soldiers were Roman Gentile soldiers as the Jews had no militia during the time when John was baptizing, ca. 30 C.E.

now separated into a community of waiting. John's baptism functions as a partial paradigm for understanding baptism in Luke-Acts. Gentiles who are baptized in Acts are also being separated out for the coming apocalypse.

Before we leave Luke's presentation of John it is crucial that we take a quick glimpse at how other gospel writers presented John so as to have a better sense of the distinctiveness of John. John's position as the announcer of Jesus is urgent to Messianic prophecy, salvation, the Church and the apocalyptic view. John is introduced by all four gospel writers, Matthew 3:1-6, Mark 1:2-6, Luke 3:1-6 and John 1: 6-7, 19-23. The synoptic gospel accounts and John's gospel each site Old Testament prophecy while portraying John the Baptist as appearing in the wilderness of Judea baptizing and calling on the Jews to repent: "A voice cries out: 'In the wilderness prepare the way of the Lord, make straight in the desert a highway for our God.' (Isa. 40:3) In this pericope all of the gospel writers are presenting John's prophetic call.

Matthew and Luke both show John preaching repentance and in all four gospels, John is shown announcing the Messiah (Matt. 3:7-12, Mk. 1:7-8, Lu. 3:7-9; 15-18. Jn. 1:24-28). In differentiating between the gospels we find that only Luke records the (historical) birth of John (Lu 1:57) to priestly parents while the others gospel writers begin with John's prophetic call. The Lukan prophetic call of John is set up early in the gospel when Zachariah, John's father, prophesies that his son would be the prophet of the Most High and would go before the Lord to prepare the people for salvation. Luke's plot creates that catalyst by which the central character, Jesus, will perform in the role of savior and deliverer of Jews and Gentiles. Hence, the institution of the Church will take place in Acts.

Returning to Luke's portrayal of John, the baptizer and prophet, it appears that Luke has John's mission end when he is imprisoned (Lu. 3:20). After John's imprisonment Jesus comes to be baptized and Luke can now focus on Jesus, the greater one whom John has said is coming to baptize with the Holy Spirit and fire (Lu. 3:16).

Luke 3:21-22
Baptism of Jesus

In addition to masses of people already baptized, Jesus too was baptized at which time we soon see the start of His ministry: "Now when all the people were baptized, and when Jesus also had been baptized and was praying, the heaven was opened up, and the Holy Spirit descended upon him in bodily form like a dove. And a voice came from heaven, You are my Son, the Beloved; with you I am well pleased." (Lu 3:21-22) Regarding the purpose of Jesus' baptism Osborn asserts: "The main purpose . . . of the baptism scene . . . is to announce the heavenly identification of Jesus as the 'Son' and (indirectly) as Yahweh's servant." [64] And, Osborne further asserts that "the presence of the Spirit marks Jesus as the chosen one. The choosing of this Jesus is God's action alone, and in this we see that baptism is not our own work, that is, our conversation or our repentance, but fundamentally the work of God."[65]

Why did Jesus submit Himself to John's baptism? The answer is in the baptism act itself, explicitly in the voice from heaven (Lu. 3:22). Many scholars over the years have experienced hermeneutical difficulty with Jesus being baptized into John's water baptism of repentance for the forgiveness of sins. Granted, if Jesus is seen in the same vein as fellow Jews then, it is easy to see how Jesus can be seen as a sinner too. But John's call was directed to all Jews with the primary focus on the identity of Jesus as shown by all four gospel writers—remission of sin was secondary.[66] Baptism marks Jesus as an apocalyptic figure in the tradition of John.

No other New Testament record of baptism is comparable with the baptism of Jesus. The voice from heaven was heard and recorded only when Jesus was baptized. The gospel writers saw Jesus' baptism as the inauguration of the messianic ministry. The first messianic act

---

[64] Kenan B. Osborne, *The Christian Sacraments of Initiation: Baptism, Confirmation, Eucharist.* 27.

[65] Ibid., 31.

[66] Ibid.

of Jesus' was His own baptism signifying solidarity with the people.[67] Cullmann asserts,

> Other Jews come to Jordan to be baptized by John for their *own* sins. Jesus, on the contrary, at the very moment when he is baptized like other people hears a voice which fundamentally declares: Thou are baptized not for thine own sins but for those of the whole people. For thou are he of whom Isaiah prophesied, that he must suffer representatively for the sins of the people. This means that Jesus is baptized in view of his death, which effects forgiveness of sins for all men. For this reason Jesus must unite himself in solidarity with his whole people, and go down himself to Jordan, that 'all righteousness might be fulfilled.'

> Thus the Baptism of Jesus points forward to the end, to the climax of his life, the Cross, in which alone all Baptism will find its fulfillment.[68]

---

[67]   G.R. Beasley-Murray, *Baptism in the New Testament* (London: Macmillan & Co Ltd, 1962), 68.

[68]   Oscar Cullmann, *Baptism in the New Testament* (London: S C M Press Ltd, 1950), 18-9. In Luke 12:50 Jesus acknowledges another kind of baptism, a stressful baptism, with which He would be baptized. This Scriptural text sets up the Lukan plot for Jesus' baptism on the Cross which Cullmann terms as a general baptism referring to Jesus death.

Luke stages Jesus' baptism as an archetype for the baptism of members of the Church to come in Acts.[69] Jesus' baptism functions as a motif for understanding baptism in Acts. And, with Jesus' baptism Luke continues to echo Jewish water rites in his presentation while increasing the emphasis on the Spirit (our topic in the next chapter).

When we examine Acts we will find that the act of the baptism of Jesus will occupy a prominent place in the Church as members will be recipients of baptism of the Holy Spirit (Acts 2:2-4; 37-42). Some scholars view Jesus' baptism as a counterpart to early Church baptism.[70] The connection between the Spirit descending upon Jesus and the beginning of Jesus' ministry is comparable to the course of events at the end of Luke and the beginning of Acts (Luke 24:46-49; Acts 1:8) and the Pentecost scene (Acts 2) reveals that the coming of the Spirit leads immediately to the expansion of the (Church) community. Tannehill states: "The coming of the Spirit to Jesus following his baptism is a crucial beginning point in the narrative whose consequences unfold as Jesus' mission develops."[71] The voice (of God) from heaven at Jesus' baptism signals that he is the Messiah and that Israel's apocalyptic eschatological expectations are being unveiled.

---

[69]   G.R. Beasley-Murray, *Baptism in the New Testament*. 63.

[70]   Ibid.

[71]   Robert C. Tannehill, *The Narrative Unity of Luke-Acts: A Literary Interpretation, Vol. 1: The Gospel according to Luke* (Philadelphia: Fortress Press, 1986), 57.

The Acts of the Apostles

Moving ahead I will look at key texts in the second part of Luke's two-volume book (Luke-Acts).[72] This volume opens with Jesus ascension into heaven, the promise of His return and spread of Apostles' witness throughout the earth. Early on in Acts Luke sets the story plot to show that Jesus left precise instructions with His Apostles while He was yet with them.

Fellowship in the Upper Room
Acts 1:4-8

In expectation of Pentecost, Jesus repeats the promise of Holy Spirit baptism to His Apostles. Here, Luke posits an understanding of baptism that goes beyond that attributed to John's water baptism. Jesus directed the Apostles to wait in Jerusalem for the promise of the Father: "you will be baptized with the Holy Spirit." (Acts 1:4-5). Luke is the only New Testament writer who specifies the exact number of days Jesus was in the midst of the Apostles during the period from the resurrection

---

[72]   I. Howard Marshall, *The Acts of the Apostles: An Introduction and Commentary* (Leicester: Inter-Varsity Press, Wm. B. Eerdmans Publishing Company, 1980), 19. Although it may appear that Luke has written two separate books this is not the case. It was common for writers in ancient times to organize one work into shorter pieces (books) and begin each with a brief introduction as Luke did with Luke-Acts. Notice Luke's introduction to Theophilus in both The Gospel of Luke and The Acts of the Apostles.

to the ascension (Acts 1:3).[73] As Jesus spoke to the Apostles they began to question Him regarding when He (the Messiah or Anointed One) would restore the kingdom to Israel (Acts 1:7).

Based on this query we see that the Apostles were anxious regarding the restoration of Israel as a monarchy and the apocalypse. Jesus reassured His Apostles that they would receive power when the Holy Spirit came; that they would be His witnesses in Jerusalem, all of Judea and Samaria, and all the earth (Acts 1:8). Here, Brawley suggests: "Supposedly, this prediction sets the pattern for the geographical extension of God's salvation and anticipates the definitive transition of the gospel from Jews (Jerusalem) to gentiles (Rome)."[74] Although Brawley has a valid point regarding the pattern for the geographical extension of God's salvation I do not quite understand how he renders the Apostles' witnessing occasions as transitioning the gospel from the Jews to the Gentiles when this event establishes that the gospel is intended for everyone on earth.

---

[73] Luke 1:3 strategically places Jesus in the company of His Apostles for forty days and tells them to remain in Jerusalem until the promise of the Father comes. The forty-day period described only in the third gospel, sets up another suspenseful Lukan plot that will connect with the promise of the Father. No doubt the entire audience will be persuaded to accept the Lukan theology linked with the arrival of the promise of the Father.

[74] Robert L. Brawley, *Luke-Acts and the Jews: Conflict, Apology, and Conciliation* Monograph Series 33 (Atlanta: Scholars Press, 1987), 28.

Promise of the Father Fulfilled
Acts 2:1-4

Luke's plot gives exceedingly strong characterization in the opening text of Acts as the audience is anticipating the grand event, the appearance of the Holy Spirit, the promise of the Father that Jesus spoke of to His Apostles (Acts 1:8). Here the milieu that Luke presents is important as we find that the time and place when the promise would be fulfilled occurred on the feast of Pentecost. Pentecost was not a new feast, but was one of three major Jewish pilgrim festivals celebrated annually for centuries during which time masses of Jews were in Jerusalem attending the festival. Luke's account of the appearance of the Holy Spirit states:

When the day of Pentecost had come, they were all together in one place. And suddenly from heaven there came a sound like the rush of a violent wind, and it filled the entire house where they were sitting. Divided tongues, as of fire, appeared among them, and a tongue rested on each of them. All of them were filled with the Holy Spirit and began to speak in other languages, as the Spirit gave them ability. (Acts 2:1-4)

The Holy Spirit appeared suddenly like a bolt from the blue.[75]

Momentarily there is a divergence from water rites in Judaism prior to the Jesus movement. However, Luke is moving the plot along in order to show that the Holy Spirit event will be part of the link between the initiation rite of the Jesus followers (the Church) and Jewish water rites prior to the Jesus movement. Here for the first time we are dealing with the manifestation of another kind of baptism, Holy Spirit baptism for which Luke has prepared us in Luke-Acts (Lu. 3:16; Acts 1:5). And so, along with John's water baptism we now see Spirit baptism introduced dramatically by Luke (Acts 2:2-5).

The motif of baptism is used here metaphorically to symbolize partakers being inundated or immersed in the power of the Holy Spirit or Spirit of God while being endowed with power from the Father (God). Turner asserts, "The community's experience of being 'baptized

---

[75] The three major Jewish pilgrim festivals celebrated annually were Passover, Sukkot and Pentecost or Shavuot. The Pentecost festival is referred to as the Feast of Weeks and Festival of Fruits (Numbers, chapter 28). There is a point to be made here that the Jews were accustomed to celebrating God on Pentecost. During second Temple times these festivals were celebrated with much gala in Jerusalem where Jews went to the Temple and offered first fruits from their fields. Pentecost was celebrated long before the occasion of the appearance of the Holy Spirit and the institution of the Church in Acts 2. The Lukan plot is strengthened when the Holy Spirit appears in the midst of this annual gala Jewish festival. The Jews were already in a mode of celebration as they presented offerings to God. We can deduce that the Apostles had to wait on the promise of power for ten days after the ascension. From the ascension of Jesus to the day of the arrival of the Holy Spirit equals fifty (Pentecost is a Greek term meaning fiftieth) days after the Passover observation. Again, the Lukan plot is crafted to make an explosive, dynamic impression on audiences.

with Holy Spirit' is . . . the fulfillment of the promise of its richly transforming 'salvation.'"[76] Pervo sees the gift of the Spirit as a gift of speech as well as serving to identify the church while giving the idea of Israel being the people of the Spirit.[77] Following this event the Apostles can now carry out their witnessing mission in Jerusalem, all of Judea and Samaria, and "to the ends of the earth." (Acts 1:8) We have just glanced at the introduction of Holy Spirit baptism and will now turn to consider how this baptism is to be observed among the new sect in Judaism, the Church.

The Appearance of the Holy Spirit
Acts 2:37-38

As we move along in Chapter Two of Acts, we find that the appearance of the Holy Spirit has caused such a great pandemonium that Peter felt the need to advise that the recipients of the Holy Spirit were not drunk. And so, Peter along with the eleven began to witness about Jesus the Messiah as he spoke to the crowd of devout Jews from every nation living in Jerusalem. Peter begin to elucidate exactly what had just taken place concluding with the statement: "Therefore let the entire house of Israel know with certainty that God has made him both

---

[76] Max Turner, "The Work of the Holy Spirit in Luke-Acts" *Word & World* 23 (2003): 146-153.

[77] Richard I. Pervo, *Luke's Story of Paul* (Minneapolis: Fortress Press, 1990), 18.

Lord and Messiah, this Jesus whom you crucified." (Acts 2:36)[78] The people, heartfelt and impacted by Peter's powerful message, began to ask Peter and the other Apostles, "Brothers, what should we do?" (Acts 2:37)

As we examine Peter's reply to the Jews it is vital that we return to the theme of Jewish water rites prior to the Jesus movement. Hence, the Lukan plot concerning the Church's baptism and Jewish water rites can be fitted together and better understood in Luke-Acts. We have previously explored baptism as an initiation into an eschatological community such as Qumran and John's (apocalyptic) water baptism. Thus, Peter instructs the crowd: "Repent, and be baptized every one of you in the name of Jesus Christ so that your sins may be forgiven; and you will receive the gift of the Holy Spirit." (Acts 2:38) Peter for the most part, duplicates the words of John the Baptist except he adds that baptism is now to be in the name of Jesus Christ, sins will now be forgiven and the gift of the Holy Spirit will be given. In the gift associated with the Jesus movement baptism, the Holy Spirit is the distinguishing feature from John's baptism.

Jewish water baptism is fused with Holy Spirit baptism as an initiation rite for the new sub sect under Judaism, the Church. With the institution of the Church the Jewish initiation rite of water baptism will remain a partial element for being inaugurated into the Church

---

[78] During Peter's message to the Jewish brethren in Acts 2:17 Peter refers to Septuagint Bible text familiar to his Jewish audience, Joel 2:28-32. (See note at Acts 2:17-21 in the NRSV Bible, pg. 2061). The text relates to the apocalyptic eschatological context of the Church.

community. The relationship of water baptism to Spirit baptism in Luke-Acts will be examined in Chapter Three. For now and in keeping with the Lukan plot we can reason that water rites in Judaism serve as background for understanding baptism in Luke-Acts.

Witnessing to All Who are Far Away
Acts 8:35-39

Beginning at Acts Chapter 8 and moving forward Luke chronicles events concerning witnessing and spreading the good news about Jesus, the Messiah. Luke has previously alerted the audience that the good news about the Messiah would be taken to ". . . the ends of the earth." (Acts 1:8) and that the "promise is . . . for all who are far away." (Acts 2:39) Prior to the story of the Ethiopian eunuch, Luke purposefully injects the story of Stephen, a martyr for the sake of the Jesus movement (Church), and introduces Saul, a vile persecutor of the Church.

Luke can now effortlessly implement the plot where the Jesus followers, except the Apostles, expeditiously leave Jerusalem and scatter into Judea and Samaria and where the good news about Jesus, the Messiah, will spread. Tannehill states,

> It is important to note, first, that the sequence in 1:8 (Jerusalem, Judea, Samaria, the end of the earth) is geographical. To be sure, the locations imply at least

three different religious groups (Jews, Samaritans, and Gentiles) who would predominate in the different locations, but these groups are represented by places that they inhabit. The Ethiopian is introduced by his geographical origin, and it is one that fittingly represents the end of the earth." [79]

Philip was the first one to take the gospel outside of Jerusalem. Wilson suggests that because of his Hellenist leadership in the Jerusalem Church he was probably prepared to move forward within greater cultural venues.[80]

This Lukan episode on witnessing and spreading the good news about Jesus is careful to orchestrate a divine command from an angel to Philip so that the listeners readily accept that the message is from God. Philip is deliberately placed alone on a wilderness road in the company of an Ethiopian eunuch.[81] They are both at the right place at the right time. For this thesis writer, I see a less than difficult plot staged for witnessing and spreading the good news about Jesus. We now

---

[79] Robert C. Tannehill, *The Narrative Unity of Luke-Acts: A Literary Interpretation, Vol. 2: The Acts of the Apostles* (Minneapolis: Fortress Press, 1990), 108.

[80] Marvin R. Wilson, *Our Father Abraham: Jewish Roots of the Christian Faith* (Grand Rapids: William B. Eerdmans Publishing Company and Center for Judaic-Christian Studies, 1989), 45.

[81] Although Luke presents the eunuch returning from a Jerusalem worship service, it is apparent that the eunuch is not a Jew based on the Torah commandment recorded at Deuteronomy 23:1 whereby a person whose testicles are crushed or whose penis is cut off cannot be admitted into the assembly of the Lord.

have Philip, a Jewish Holy Spirit filled missionary from the Jerusalem Church, and a foreigner returning from a Jerusalem worship event and reading Hebrew Scripture from Isaiah.

After the man finished reading the text he interrogated Philip about the identity of the person in the text. It is apparent that the Ethiopian was eager to believe and accept Philip's hermeneutical presentation. We are not told exactly what words Philip used to describe the good news about Jesus. It is clear however that Philip had to have explained the Messianic fulfillment in such a manner as to convince the Ethiopian of the whole experience of the appearance of the Holy Spirit at Pentecost. No doubt Philip explained the Holy Spirit as a gift to the world for all who are far away (Acts 2:39). Rather than modern Ethiopia, the eunuch was from what is now known as Sudan.[82]

Based on Luke's portrayal of the Pentecost event, Philip had to have used unambiguous dialogue while stressing that the Holy Spirit was for those separated out, for those awaiting the end times Peter referred to in his Pentecost message (Acts 2:19-21). If Philip had been less than articulate in his presentation to the Ethiopian it is apparent that the Ethiopian would not have comprehended the message. Marshall says, "Philip must have spoken to him along the lines of Peter's sermon in Acts 2, especially verse 38, regarding the appropriate response to

---

[82] I. Howard Marshall, *The Acts of the Apostles; An Introduction and Commentary.* (Grand Rapids: William B. Eerdmans Publishing Company, 1980), 165.

the . . . message."[83] Furthermore, Marshall continues to describe Philip's conversation with the Ethiopian: "Clearly his first step was to show that Jesus was the person who fulfilled the prophecy."[84] In order for the Ethiopian, a first time hearer of the good news about Jesus, to comprehend Philip's witness Philip must have emphasized the need for the Holy Spirit and water baptism as a prerequisite to be inducted into the community awaiting the second coming.

In this writer's view the essence of Acts 8:35-39 is that the good news regarding Jesus was preached and by faith the Ethiopian received Philip's witness. Thus, an Ethiopian foreigner was baptized in water by Philip and became a part of the Church community. The same kind of dynamism seen at Pentecost when the Holy Spirit arrived occurred when Philip was suddenly caught away from the scene by the Spirit after he had baptized the eunuch and when the eunuch went away rejoicing. We do not know whether it included tongues. It is not clear why Luke does not state that the eunuch received the Holy Spirit. It is this writer's opinion that Luke has set the stage for the likelihood of his audience to accept that the Holy Spirit including speaking in tongues, followed the eunuch's water baptism. Philip landed about twenty-two miles north of Gaza where the baptism had been conducted. Marshall suggests that sufficient evidence does not exist to show exactly what methodology

---

[83] Ibid., 162.

[84] Ibid., 164.

was used for the baptism, immersion or pouring water over the eunuch while he stood in the shallow water.[85]

As insightful as Marshall's comment may be, it does not bear on the issue at hand: Water was used to baptize the eunuch. Water baptism of the Ethiopian eunuch played a vital role in affirming a major motif in Luke-Acts, water baptism. (e.g., proselyte baptism, John's baptism, etc.). Philip was among the first to spread the good news of the Messiah outside of the Jerusalem Church. It is this writer's view that the Ethiopian was immersed in the water by Philip; that water was likely plentiful along the Mediterranean coastal area where these two men had their encounter. It seems that for the most part, New Testament writers thought that baptisms were to be conducted in natural bodies of water; such as, streams, rivers, lakes and the sea.[86]

Like the Pentecost experience, water baptism and Spirit baptism represent the complete initiation process for becoming a part of the Church in waiting.[87] The Lukan message is that if water baptism is

---

[85]   Ibid., 165.

[86]   S. Anita Stauffer, "Cultural Settings of Architecture for Baptism in the Early Church" in *Worship and Culture in Dialogue,* ed. S. Anita Stauffer. (Geneva: Lutheran World Federation, 1994), 57.

[87]   Here Luke does not recreate precisely the occurrence of the Holy Spirit appearance at the Pentecost celebration. He does not state that the eunuch spoke in another language. Hence, here we can assume that Luke does not make this a requirement for people being initiated into the Church. The eunuch went on his way rejoicing because he was filled with the Holy Spirit. Otherwise, what would be Luke's purpose for including the episode in Acts 8:35-39 in support of witnessing and spreading the good news about the Messiah?

received then God will send the gift of the Holy Spirit. Thus, we see the eunuch's outcome: he was the first non-Jew to be saved in Acts. Luke continues to make use of echoes of Jewish (purification) water rites as background for understanding baptism presented in Luke-Acts. Luke presents yet another baptism scenario as we continue to follow the Lukan story of the spread of the good news of Jesus Christ, the Messiah and the spreading of the Church.

Gentiles are Saved the Same as Jews
Acts 10:44-47; 11:14-17

Thus far as word concerning the Messiah is spreading abroad we see that water baptism and Spirit baptism have occurred with Jews and Samaritans who accepted the message (Acts 2:1-11; 37-39; 8:4-17; 35-39). I will now study another Lukan episode where a new group is initiated into the Church community. Here the plot reveals the Holy Spirit infilling of Gentiles the same as Jews on Pentecost (2:38). But, Luke presents this scenario in reverse order: first the receipt of the gift of the Holy Spirit and speaking in tongues is witnessed and, second water baptism takes place. Nonetheless, the story continues to include witnessing and spreading the good news of Jesus, the Messiah and people are saved (Joel 2:32; Acts 2:40-47).

Luke again gives divine characterization to the environment in this plot: an angel of God delivers a message to Cornelius while he was praying (Acts 10:30) and a voice from heaven (Luke 3:22; Acts 10:11, 13-15) speaks to Peter in a vision. Peter journeyed northwest of Jerusalem to Lydda and then on to Joppa (Acts 9:32-43). While in Joppa, Peter stayed at the home of Simon, the tanner. During his stay, Peter was praying and fell into a trance. In the dream Peter was told three times by a voice from heaven to kill and eat "all kinds of four-footed creatures and reptiles and birds of the air." (Acts 10:12)[88] Initially, Peter did not understand the meaning of the dream. In the meantime, Cornelius was directed by "an angel of God" (Acts10:3) to gather men and travel to Joppa where he would find Peter at the home of Simon, a tanner.

We now have the formula for a grand Lukan plot. Again, Luke places two main characters together: Peter, an evangelist and Church leader from the Jerusalem Church and Cornelius, a God-fearing Gentile (Acts 10:2) who has not yet heard the salvation message about the Messiah. Both men obeyed their divine messages. Even though Peter and Cornelius both received divine messages Tannehill asserts, "there is some reflection on human factors in the receipt of divine messages. Cornelius' vision occurs while he is at prayer (10:30) . . . a vision in which Peter is commanded to eat comes to him when he is . . . also

---

[88]   It is implied here that there are no clean animals. Only God could have caused Peter, a Jew, to consider eating profane animals as Peter was a product of Judaism, a religion where dietary laws did not permit eating four-footed creatures, reptiles or birds of the air because they were considered unclean (Leviticus 11, Deuteronomy 14).

praying 10:9)"[89] Peter, Cornelius and Cornelius' entourage meet in Joppa.

The heart of the theme of baptism in this instance now begins: Peter begins to speak to the group: "I truly understand that God shows no partiality, but in every nation anyone who fears him and does what is right is acceptable to him." (Acts 10:34-35) Allen explains that "In regard to the relationship between Luke's religious vision and the religions of the Gentiles, Luke keeps faith with Judaism by stating that God is universal and impartial."[90] Marshall on the other hand states it thusly: "This does not mean that salvation is possible apart from the atonement wrought by Jesus Christ, but rather that on the basis of his death and resurrection the gospel is offered to all people who are willing to receive it and recognize their need of it."[91]

As Peter spoke the Holy Spirit fell on the group around him and they spoke in tongues and praised God. The Jews who accompanied Peter were dumbfounded by what they saw and heard: Gentiles receiving the gift of the Holy Spirit. Luke organized this event in such a way as to guarantee that his associates witnessed the Gentiles receiving the Holy Spirit. Afterwards Peter ordered the Gentiles to be

---

[89]   Robert C. Tannehill, *The Narrative Unity of Luke-Acts: A Literary Interpretation, Vol. 2: The Acts of the Apostles.* 129.

[90]   Ronald J. Allen, "The Story of the Church According to 'Luke' The Acts of the Apostles" in *Chalice Introduction to the New Testament.* 205.

[91]   I. Howard Marshall, *The Acts of the Apostles: An Introduction and Commentary,* 189-90.

baptized. This episode continues to include Holy Spirit baptism and water baptism as Luke continues to tell the story of the spread of the Church from Jerusalem to Judea, Samaria and the end of the earth (Acts 1:8). One element of this new initiation practice is similar only in part compared to Jewish water rites prior to the Jesus movement and that is the part dealing with the act of water baptism only. Luke emphasizes that the other part, receiving the gift of the Holy Spirit, is necessary for those separated out and awaiting kingdom restoration. John's water baptism was a call to repentance in preparation for the baptism of the Holy Spirit which has come and is now available to all who receive it.

John's water baptism had insufficient power as it was preparatory pointing towards power through the gift of the Holy Spirit. Regarding water baptism, Marshall asserts:

> Baptism had become the outward sign of reception into the people of God. It was the sign of cleansing from sin, and so of forgiveness (2:38), but at the same time it was seen as the outward accompaniment and sign of being inwardly baptized by the Spirit; the latter did not replace water-baptism. Since the Gentiles had been baptized with the Holy Spirit, it followed that they were eligible to be baptized with water.[92]

---

[92] Ibid., 194.

The only question that a true witness could have asked when the Gentiles received the gift of the Holy Spirit prior to baptism was asked by Peter, "Can anyone withhold the water for baptizing these people who have received the Holy Spirit just as we have?" (Acts10:47)

Afterwards Peter returned to the Jerusalem Church and gave a report of all that had transpired regarding the Gentiles' salvation (Acts 11:14). We find that this is Luke's second report of a Gentile conversion, the Ethiopian eunuch was the first (Acts 8:35-39). Luke's world of the good news about the Messiah continues to be spread to the end of the earth (Acts 1:8) as we look at another episode.

Recipients of John's Water Baptism
Receive the Holy Spirit
Acts 19:1-6

Before getting into the core of Paul's encounter with twelve recipients of John's baptism, I will take a quick look at Saul's initiation into "the Way" (Acts 9:2) in order to capture the dominant dual roles in which Luke casts Saul (Paul) in Acts. In Chapter One I referred to Saul as a persecutor of the Church (Acts 8:3). In Acts 9 Saul is converted and initiated into "the Way" and becomes the lead person to spread the gospel of Jesus Christ to the Gentiles (Acts 9:15). By the time Acts 19:1-6 is recorded much has happened in the life of Saul since he was first introduced by Luke (Acts 8:3). Luke continues to bring great drama into his storytelling. For example, Saul was converted through a dramatic encounter with the Lord: "suddenly a light from heaven flashed around him. He fell to the ground and heard a voice." (Acts 9:3-4) and received direction from God.

Again, Luke uses the methodology of a dream to develop the plot for two main characters, Saul and Ananias, a disciple in Damascus. These two men meet and execute the plan of God which was that Saul would regain his eyesight, receive the gift of the Holy Spirit and be baptized (Acts 9:10-19). Ananias laid hands on Saul and said, "'Brother Saul, the Lord Jesus, who appeared to you on your way here, has sent me so that you may regain your sight and be filled with the Holy Spirit.'" (Acts 9:17) Luke has hearers presume that since the scale-like mass fell from Saul's eyes that Saul is empowered with the Holy Spirit simultaneously. Hence, Saul can now witness and spread the gospel too. Without delay thereafter in Damascus Saul started to declare Jesus in the synagogues saying, "'He is the Son of God.'" (Acts 9:20)

Saul amazed the Jews with his witness as he proved that Jesus was the Messiah (Acts 9:22). The disciples at Jerusalem however continued to be afraid of Saul because of his past mission to persecute "the Way." In Jerusalem Saul was under the threat of death and believers helped him eventually return to his hometown, Tarsus. Later Barnabas traveled to Tarsus picked up Saul and they traveled to Antioch together. Their abode was in Antioch for about a year where they taught many people in the Church (Acts 11:25-26). While a group at the Antioch Church where worshipping the Lord and fasting the Holy Spirit spoke: "Set apart for me Barnabas and Saul for the work to which I have called them." (Acts 13:2) For some unknown reason we find that Luke begins to refer to Saul as Paul (Acts 13:9). Paul begins to travel extensively on what are referred to as (witnessing) missionary journeys spreading the message about Jesus, the Messiah.

As we move forward in this writing we find that Luke places Paul in the interior regions of Ephesus (Acts 19:1). Prior to arriving at this particular site in Ephesus Paul traveled extensively preaching the message of Jesus in synagogues and assisting disciples in various places (e.g., Syria, Cenchreae, Ephesus, Galatia and Phrygia (Acts 18:18-25).[93] Luke appears eager to unravel the episode beginning in Acts 19. Luke depicts Paul as being deeply passionate in his witness about the Messiah to men he just met. This is evident in Paul's terse questioning of these disciples at the outset of the meeting: "Did you receive the Holy Spirit when you became believers." (Acts 19:2)[94]

To momentarily deviate from the baptism of these disciples we will look at some events just prior to the meeting of Paul and the

---

[93] Previously Paul had briefly spoken to the Jews in the synagogue in Ephesus but he did not tarry there (Acts 18:19).

[94] In Acts 9:15 Luke alerts the audience that God had chosen Saul to bring God's name before Gentiles, kings and Israel. When we find Paul at Ephesus questioning disciples he encounters for the first time, Paul is keenly aware of his obligation as God's emissary for Christ. Here, Paul's zealousness about getting the correct Messianic message to every person is paramount.

disciples. In this thesis writer's view in Acts 18 Luke sets up the plot for what transpires in Acts 19:1-6. In Acts 18 Luke places Apollos a Jew, at Ephesus after Paul had left (Ephesus). Consequently, Apollos would not have heard Paul preaching in the synagogue at Ephesus (Acts 18:19). I suggest that it is possible these disciples were limited to hearing Apollos teaching John's baptism in Ephesus; therefore, this is all they would have known when they later encountered Paul at Ephesus in Acts 19:1. Moreover, it is my view that although Luke describes Apollos as knowledgeable in the Way of the Lord, Apollos apparently grossly misunderstood the pivotal part of the message, the bestowal of the Holy Spirit on believers after being baptized in water.

Luke presents Apollos as an eloquent man stirred with enthusiasm who taught precisely the things of Jesus though he knew only John's baptism. Tannehill asserts that "In v. 25 the narrator refers to 'the spirit' in connection with Apollos' speech. There is debate whether this refers to his personal temperament . . . or to the effect of the Holy Spirit on his speech."[95] Despite Tannehill's statement concerning a debate over one's own temperament versus the effect of the Holy Spirit, Luke states that Apollos knew only John's baptism (v. 26). Therefore, it is highly unlikely that in v. 25 Luke was referring to the effect of the Holy Spirit in Apollos' speech.

---

[95] Robert C. Tannehill, *The Narrative Unity of Luke-Acts: A Literary Interpretation, Vol. 2: The Acts of the Apostles.* 232.

It was only after other believers at Ephesus, Priscilla and Aquila, instructed Apollos in the message of Jesus, the Messiah, that Apollos began to teach the message of Jesus thoroughly and completely (Acts 18:24-26). It is thus conceivable to this writer that at some point these twelve disciples had heard Apollos speak only of John's water baptism of repentance while they were in Ephesus. Sometime later we learn that the twelve men whom Paul met revealed to Paul that they had not even heard of the Holy Spirit (Acts 19:2). Paul seized the opportunity to baptize these disciples "in the name of the Lord Jesus. When Paul had laid his hands on them, the Holy Spirit came upon them, and they spoke in tongues and prophesied." (Acts 19:5-7).

Again Luke shows the Holy Spirit being received by the disciples at Ephesus only after Paul laid hands on them. Buse suggests that some usually link the gift of the Spirit with laying on of hands when they deny the correlation between baptism and the bestowal of the Holy Spirit.[96] Buse further suggests that the link between the Holy Spirit and laying on of hands was developed later than the ancient Jerusalem church.[97] Johnson on the other hand, suggests that situations such as recorded in

---

[96]   S.I. Buse, Baptism in the Acts of the Apostles" in *Christian Baptism: A Fresh Attempt to Understand the Rite in Terms of Scripture, History and Theology*, ed. A. Gilmore, intro. E.A. Payne. (Chicago: Judson Press, 1959), 118.

[97]   Ibid., 122.

Acts 8:14-17 and 19-1-7 relative to a hand laying rite, do not represent a typical pattern. Instead it applies to specific and unique occasions.[98]

This practice was not done when the Holy Spirit first appeared at the Pentecost celebration nor was it mentioned in Acts in some other instances: Acts 2:38; 8:38-39; 10:44-48. I do not interpret the practice of laying on of hands as anything that Luke tried to develop as a permanent rite mandatory for being initiated into the Church community. Otherwise, Luke the persuasive storyteller would have shown this practice consistently throughout Acts as he did the water baptismal rite.

In this chapter we have examined water baptism in Luke-Acts in comparison to Jewish water rites. The next chapter will look at the relationship of water baptism to Spirit baptism in Luke-Acts.

---

[98] Maxwell Johnson, *The Rites of Christian Initiation: Their Evolution and Interpretation*. 25.

CHAPTER THREE

Reflections on Water Baptism and
Spirit Baptism for Today

In this chapter I will track one phase of the development of the
Christian Church and Christianity as interpreted by Luke in his two-
volume work. I will discuss the connection of water baptism to Holy
Spirit baptism in Luke-Acts. Throughout this thesis I have spoken
explicitly concerning ancient religious practices using water rites and
symbolisms. I will now discuss religious practices involving water rites
in the early Jesus movement and in the early Church as presented
in Luke-Acts as connected to the Holy Spirit. What, if any, is the
relationship of water and Spirit baptism in Luke-Acts?

After an examination of key texts on water baptism and Spirit
baptism recorded in Luke-Acts I have found that there is a definite

relationship between water and Spirit baptism (Lu. 3:3-22; Acts 1:4-8; 2:1-4, 37:39; 8:35-39; 10:44-47; 11:14-16 and 19:1-6). In order to properly discuss this relationship I will look at the role of the Holy Spirit in the Church community as well as the symbolism of the water element in the process of forming a complete relationship between the believer, the eschatological community and God. In Acts 2:38 the Holy Spirit is described as a gift, a gift available to everyone who repents and is baptized in the name of Jesus Christ for the forgiveness of sins. Upon receipt of this gift Jews and Gentiles are empowered.

This gift of the Holy Spirit is apocalyptic eschatological in nature as it empowers the community of God to maintain until the return of Jesus who will rule and restore the kingdom of God on earth. Nolland asserts, "the Holy Spirit is also witness (5:32), and Luke will understand this in terms of the tangible presence of the power of God in the church and the individual Christian (Acts 2:6-12 [cf. v 33], 43 [cf. v 47]; 4:13, 16 etc.)."[99]

This apocalyptic view has a direct linkage with John's baptism from the perspective that John was a prophet and intermediary who went before the Messiah and gave hope of salvation to the Jews (Luke 1:69, 77). John's call to repentance was preparatory in view of Jesus' coming and those who received John's baptism were prepared to welcome Jesus, the Anointed One. However, John's water baptism ritual was ineffective without repentance. Regarding John's baptism Nolland explains,

---

[99]   John Nolland, *Luke 1:1-9:20 Word Biblical Commentary*, Vol 35A. 153.

The connection between baptism and forgiveness of sins is thus to be understood in relation to the OT imagery of a divine washing. In line with OT prophetic symbolism . . . John used the waters of the Jordan to effect the eschatologically promised washing away of sin. His self-depreciating reference to the coming one (Luke 3:16-17) indicates, however, that he was conscious of being unable to deliver all that such an eschatological cleansing implied."[100]

The Anointed One, Jesus, would restore the kingdom of Israel and deliver a thorough and complete divine cleansing through the gift of Holy Spirit baptism (Acts 1:7-8). Hence, Jesus came and His identity as Messiah was made known (Lu. 3:21-22; 24:44-47). Luke describes Jesus as Savior (Lu. 1:47, 69-79; 2:11).

Jesus departed from earth (Lu. 24:51) and sent the Holy Spirit; thus, Jesus will return to save and rule the kingdom of God. Allen asserts that the emphasis of the Spirit in Acts . . . "may be for the purpose of kindling hope in the midst of the delay."[101] Further Allen claims that "The gospel reveals the identity and purpose of Jesus Christ as divine agent through whom the reign of God is manifest."[102]

---

[100] Ibid., 141-2.
[101] Ronald J. Allen, "The Story of the Church According to 'Luke' The Acts of the Apostles" in *Chalice Introduction to the New Testament*. 203.
[102] Ibid., 199.

A relationship between water baptism and Spirit baptism in Luke-Acts is at times implicit (Lu. 3:16; Acts 1:4; 8:35-39). Other times the relationship is demonstrated explicitly as hearers of the Messianic message respond and are baptized and receive the gift of the Holy Spirit (Acts 2:1-4, 37-41; 8:17; 10:44-47; 11:14-17; 19:1-6).[103] Recipients then become part of the Church community awaiting the return of Jesus (Acts 2:44-47). The work of the Holy Spirit is characteristically eschatological as it empowers the Church community to witness as they go forth. And so, water baptism alone is an inadequate physical act and therefore is not an end in or of itself.

The relationship between water baptism and Holy Spirit baptism is most fully presented at Pentecost at the initial emergence of the Spirit. Regarding the Pentecost Spirit relationship Nolland asserts, "The Pentecostal Spirit . . . confers a certain intimacy of relationship with God and strengthens for a resolute stand and witness for Christ (Acts 1:8; 4:31; Luke 12:12; 24:48-49)."[104] This gift is what Jesus spoke of to His disciples: "But you will receive power when the Holy Spirit has come upon you . . ." (Acts 1:8).

Salvation is achieved through water baptism and Holy Spirit baptism recorded by Luke; thus, a relationship exists between the two. It is my view that key texts mentioned in Luke and discussed in this writing

---

[103] Luke does not mandate a specific order in which water baptism and Spirit baptism must occur.

[104] John Nolland, *Luke 1:1-9:20 Word Biblical Commentary*, Vol 35A. 153.

have not shown explicitly that Holy Spirit baptism can be brought to fruition without water baptism (Acts 2:1-4, 37-41; 8:17; 10:44-47; 11:14-17; 19:1-6). I therefore support the hypothesis that one cannot receive Spirit baptism without water baptism. The reverse is also true.[105]

In order to fully support the relationship of water baptism to Spirit baptism it should be understood that water used in respect to sanctification and purification by the Hebrew people for millennia symbolized a washing away of the ungodly or profane. This was a practice that was used as a ritual purification rite upon God's commandment in the Torah (Leviticus). Also, water was used to prepare people for the coming apocalypse (e.g., John's baptism, Qumran water rituals). And so, proselyte baptism, John's baptism and other primeval water rites common among the Jews before the Jesus movement and the coming of the Holy Spirit, were a means of sanctification and/or purification before God and, to Luke, signaled the coming of the apocalypse. In Chapter One I looked at Eliade's comments on water: in initiation rituals immersion in water symbolizes a total regeneration, a rebirth. This same principle of rebirth can be applied to water baptism when it interconnects with Holy Spirit baptism.

Returning to Luke's presentation of baptism in Luke-Acts I have found that Luke does not systematically establish one fixed archetypical

---

[105] John's apocalyptic eschatological water baptism alone was insufficient. The ritual of John's water baptism was preparatory awaiting Spirit baptism which arrived at the Pentecost celebration (ca. 30 C.E.). The baptisms then were fused together as one unit which is necessary for initiation into the Church.

methodology for being saved and initiated into the apocalyptic Christian manner of life. Luke does however tell of the necessity of both kinds of baptism. In his presentation of baptism Luke carefully knitted together a convincing and persuasive picture of the need for John's water baptism and Holy Spirit baptism (Lu. 3:16; Acts 1:8). In Acts Luke sets the plot where water baptism and Spirit baptism with speaking in tongues occurs (Acts 2:4; 10:44-48; 19:1-6). Luke omits discussion of Spirit baptism in the incident of the Ethiopian eunuch whom Philip baptized in water; however, it is inferred by the fact that Luke tells us the eunuch went on his way rejoicing (Acts 8:35-39). Thus, the reader is left to deduce that the Ethiopian received Spirit baptism.

Contemporary Reflections: Implications for Today

How does the contemporary Christian Church fit into the belief system recorded in Luke-Acts? We've examined key texts regarding water baptism while exploring Holy Spirit baptism as well. In the Introduction of this thesis I acknowledged that many churches today think they follow practices (e.g., water baptism) and belief systems of the first century church. While continuing to explore the relationship of water baptism to Spirit baptism in the Christian Church I will peek at two contemporary Christian perceptions, Pentecostal and Charismatic, using excerpts from an article by Koo Dong Yun on water baptism and Spirit baptism.[106]

For centuries the Christian Church has experienced dissimilar understandings of baptism embedded in an assortment of doctrinal traditions and Bible hermeneutics. The Pentecostals saw much tumult near the turn of the twentieth century when the Azuza Street revival in Los Angeles broke out and spread across the United States. The Charismatic movement evolved from the early Pentecostal movement and embarked on Roman Catholicism and mainline Protestantism (e.g., Presbyterian, Lutheran and Anglican) during the 1960s.[107] Yun asserts that both Pentecostal and Charismatic experiences symbolize an experience of 'being filled with/in the Holy Spirit.'[108]

The Charismatic experience of infilling of the Spirit emphasizes signs of various charisms (e.g., prophecy, healing, and teaching) as well as glossolalia (tongues).[109] On the other hand, the Pentecostal experience of being filled with the Spirit is linked directly with speaking

---

[106] Koo dong Yun, "Water Baptism and Spirit Baptism: Pentecostals and Lutherans in Dialogue." *Dialog: A Journal of Theology* 43:4 (Winter 2004): 344-351.

[107] Ibid.

[108] Ibid. Yun refers to Pentecostals led by William Seymour during the 1906 Azuza Street revival as "Classical" Pentecostals. The correct term used to describe this group is "Apostolic" Pentecostals. Christ Temple Apostolic Faith Assembly in Indianapolis, Indiana is a product of the historical Azuza Street revival. Christ Temple is often referred to as the 'mother church' stemming from the Apostolic Pentecostal movement. G.T. Haywood was the first pastor of the church and leaves a strong legacy of doctrinal teachings on "Oneness."

[109] Koo Dong Yun, "Water Baptism and Spirit Baptism: Pentecostals and Lutherans in Dialogue." *Dialog: A Journal of Theology*: 344-351.

in tongues (glossolalia) and glossolalia is considered evidence of the infilling of the Spirit. Charismatic Christians however embrace Spirit baptism without glossolalia. Yun suggested that during the first half of the twentieth century extremist Classical Pentecostal Christians (Apostolic Pentecostals) taught that salvation was not possible without Spirit baptism accompanied by speaking in tongues.

In the Apostolic Pentecostal Christian Church today this same doctrine of Spirit baptism accompanied by speaking in tongues is still taught for the legitimization of salvation. In other words, an individual who has been baptized in water but does not speak in tongues has undergone only part of the process for initiation into the Christian Church. Whenever that person speaks in tongues he/she is considered saved. Yun suggests that Luke presumes two baptisms: water and Spirit baptism.[110] Admittedly, it seems that Yun and other scholars can say that Luke presumes two baptisms but another issue needs to be considered; specifically, when Spirit baptism comes into being, water baptism is not eliminated by Luke (Acts 2:41; 8:35-39; 10:47-48). Hence, it can be construed that a relationship between water baptism and Holy Spirit baptism is present.

In my view Barth's theology on the subject of the baptism experience succinctly encapsulates the relationship between water baptism and Spirit baptism, two forms of one baptism:

---

[110]   Ibid.

(1) a baptism with the Holy Spirit . . . and (2) baptism with water. For Barth, Spirit baptism designates a divine subjective change, bringing about human freedom, so that humans in turn are enabled to respond to God in water baptism. Thus, Spirit baptism makes possible and demands water baptism. According to Barth, one should not separate Spirit baptism and water baptism. Nor should one confuse them. Barth writes, 'Only as the two are seen together in differentiated unity can one understand them.' The two forms of one baptism remain the indispensable elements in laying the foundation of the Christian life.[111]

Spirit baptism and water baptism are akin to marriage whereby two people are united and become as one unit. With this unity the Church is empowered for witnessing and spreading the good news about the Messiah, Jesus Christ.

As I move ahead I will continue to examine practices and beliefs of Pentecostals and Charismatics in the contemporary church. Yun suggests that all except "Oneness" Pentecostals embrace two separate baptisms: Spirit baptism and water baptism.[112] In Apostolic Pentecostal

---

[111] Karl Barth, *Church Dogmatics, vol. IV4 The Doctrine of Reconciliation*. eds. G.W. Bromiley, T.F. Torrance, trans. G.W. Bromiley. (London: T&T Clark, 1969), 41.

[112] Koo Dong Yun, "Water Baptism and Spirit Baptism: Pentecostals and Lutherans in Dialogue." 344-351.

assemblies (under the auspices of the Pentecostal Assemblies of the World, Inc.) the Oneness doctrine is taught. Many Christians suppose that Oneness doctrine eliminates the conceptual reality of the Father, Son, and Holy Spirit. It does not. Oneness doctrine simply teaches that it was Jesus, the Christ, who satisfied the OT prophecy of Anointed One, Savior and Redeemer for all humanity; that it was Jesus only who paid the price.

The Apostolic Pentecostal teaching on water baptism in the name of Jesus is clearly in line with the pericope written by Luke: "There is salvation in no one else, for there is no other name under heaven given among mortals by which we must be saved." (Acts 4:12)[113] There is no biblical record of any person being baptized, as many believers are today, using the Trinitarian formula. Many Christians use Matt. 28:19 as support for embracing a Trinitarian formula by which baptism should be administered: in the Name of the Father, Son and Holy Spirit. The Lukan Christians spoke of their baptism as being in the name of

---

[113]   Frequently Apostolic Pentecostal Christians are mocked and negatively characterized as "Jesus Only" and "Oneness" weirdoes. Yet, the Bible directly endorses "Jesus Only" and "Oneness" views as stated in NT writings (e.g., Luke 4:12, Acts 2:38 and Colossians 2:9). Also Apostolic Pentecostal Christians are referred to as strange because they speak in other tongues which they interpret as the evidence of one receiving the gift of the Holy Spirit following repentance and water baptism in the Name of Jesus Christ. Speaking in tongues is also a practice mentioned in NT writings (e.g., Luke 1:4; Acts 10:46; 19:1-6).

Jesus.[114] Admittedly, there are three manifestations or titles referenced in vs. 19 but, the Apostles clearly always baptized in the name of Jesus from the day of Pentecost forward.

The three manifestations of God in the Apostolic Pentecostal church are explained thusly:

> . . . He is 'Father' in His relationship to His Creation; He is 'Son' in His redemptive role in saving the human element of His creation; He is 'Holy Ghost' in His sanctifying and preserving the indwelt believer; but His name is One-Jesus.[115]

This teaching in my view clearly aligns with Peter's message on the day of Pentecost when the Holy Spirit appeared (Acts 2:38). In response to the Jewish crowd's question regarding which way they should precede Peter said: ". . . Repent, and be baptized every one of you in the name of Jesus Christ . . ." In a capsule, this is the "Oneness" teaching.

Apostolic Pentecostals teach that there are three manifestations of God: Father, Son and Holy Spirit; however, this is not interpreted to

---

[114] Lars Hartman, *"Into the Name of the Lord Jesus:" Baptism in the Early Church,* (Edinburgh: T&T Clark LTD, 1997), 37.

[115] Organizational Manual *2004 Minute Book.* Indianapolis: Pentecostal Assemblies of the World, Inc., 2005.

mean three separate persons.[116] Another pericope that expresses the Apostolic Pentecostal Oneness doctrine wholeheartedly is: "For in him the whole fullness of deity dwells bodily." (Col. 2:9) Though not speaking of the "Oneness" doctrine per se, Hartman asserts: "Luke, when writing Acts, hardly thought that there was any difference in the meaning of the different formulae. But how then to explain the variety? Possibly Luke knew of several forms actually in use, in which case the differences could depend on tradition."[117]

In the matter of baptizing in the name of Jesus (as Apostolic Pentecostals do) and not contradicting the existence of different traditions Hartman asserts:

> Luke encountered the phrase 'in the name (of somebody)'
> in Mark (see e.g. Mark 9.37ff/Luke 9.48f); the same

---

[116] Most denominational churches criticize the Apostolic Pentecostal Church for not carrying out the practice of water baptism in the name of the Father, Son and Holy Spirit (Matt. 28:19). Apostolic Pentecostals baptize in the name of Jesus Christ (Acts 2:38). Apostolic Pentecostals view Father, Son and Holy Spirit as titles but the name associated with these titles is Jesus Christ. Father, Son and Holy Spirit is a Trinitarian concept (Blessed Trinity) developed by Tertullian about two hundred years after the Church was instituted. Neither the OT nor the NT teaches a Trinitarian doctrine. The Hebrew Bible was the Bible Jesus used during His ministry. The Jews during Jesus' time would have considered a Trinitarian concept as heresy the same as the NT writers. It is no different today. The Jews composed the audience on the day of Pentecost when the Holy Spirit appeared. Deuteronomy 6:4 was the commandment by which the Jews lived: the Lord alone was their Lord, one God. This commandment was not eliminated.

[117] Lars Hartman, *"Into the Name of the Lord Jesus:" Baptism in the Early Church.* 37.

holds true of 'because of the name (of somebody)' (Mark 13.6/Luke 21.8). But more importantly, he knows of them from the Septuagint. There they are also used of acts of worship: e.g. somebody prays 'in (God's) name' (Deut 10.8) or brings a sacrifice 'because of (God's) name' (Mal1.11). Now, it is well known that Luke wants to keep a biblical style.

. . . the different forms 'in the name (of somebody)' and 'because of the name (of somebody)' are well suited to Luke's authorial techniques.[118]

This clearly supports that Luke does not specify one certain formulae. Again, Luke's writing style is apparent. Although Luke does not explicitly develop a doctrine of "Oneness," Luke's views are at least sympathetic to the doctrine of "Oneness" especially with respect to baptism which is only in the name of Jesus Christ in Acts. Following my study of Luke-Acts, I support this gospel writer's view on the subject.

Based on Luke's biblical, historiographical and authorial techniques it is my opinion that the age old feud on "Oneness" and "Trinitarianism" may be simply a matter of semantics. It is my observation that many contemporary Christians do not understand the exegetics and the

---

[118] Ibid., 38-9

ancient literary style of the Bible but they do believe that there is only one God (Deut. 6:4).

Returning to my discussion on Apostolic Pentecostal teachings, I will state my final comments concerning Yon's article on water and Spirit baptism. Legitimacy and efficacy of water baptism in mainline churches was questioned by Pentecostals during the first half of the twentieth century.[119] This is still questioned by Apostolic Pentecostals. Apostolic Pentecostals continue to question water baptism separated from Holy Spirit baptism and speaking in tongues in mainline churches. Again, water baptism must be accompanied with Holy Spirit baptism in Apostolic Pentecostal Christian churches in order to be birthed into the Church. In this writing I have been able only to begin to inform readers of a few real insights concerning Apostolic Pentecostal and Charismatic church teachings regarding the infilling of the Holy Spirit and being initiated into the contemporary Church. I will now look at what impact this study may have on the Church today.

Multiple Relationships between Receiving Water Baptism and the Spirit

In this thesis I investigated some key texts in Luke-Acts on water baptism and Spirit baptism. I set out to elucidate what I see as a flawed

---

119   Koo Dong Yun, "Water Baptism and Spirit Baptism: Pentecostals and Lutherans in Dialogue." *Dialog: A Journal of Theology:* 344-351.

understanding of the origins of water baptism in the Christian Church today. Some would ask: what does it matter? Admittedly, as with many misunderstood and/or ambiguous Bible doctrines, there is always the option of continuing to embrace embedded traditions as usual. I do not however agree with this option. The better we understand the concept of ancient Jewish water rites for example, the better we will understand the roots/origins of water baptism used in the Church today.

From this writer's perspective it is basic that practicing contemporary Christians understand origins of NT Bible beliefs and practices so that they will better understand the underpinnings and exegesis of ancient texts. Luke has recorded instances of baptism which I have previously examined in Chapter Two using a sampling of key texts. I will now evaluate those texts and hone in on Luke's prerequisite for being initiated into the Church community. I will then discuss the primeval Jewish practice of water baptism which the contemporary Christian church adapted from the Jewish people at the inception of the Church. In conclusion, I will offer some considerations or suggestions for adapting a better understanding of water baptism and Spirit baptism in Luke's NT writings. We will begin with that day of Pentecost when the Holy Spirit arrived and dynamism erupted:

> And suddenly from heaven there came a sound like the
> rush of a violent wind, and it filled the entire house
> where they were sitting. Divided tongues, as of fire

appeared among them, and a tongue rested on each of them. All of them were filled with the Holy Spirit and began to speak in other languages, as the Spirit gave them ability.[120]

In this pericope Luke portrays that all were filled with the Holy Spirit and spoke in other languages as enabled by the Spirit. Jews from many nations (e.g., Parthians, Medes, Mesopotamians, Egyptians, etc.) were present, yet each nationality heard and understood the native language of the other. Continuing in the same chapter Luke states:

Peter said to them, Repent, and be baptized every one of you in the name of Jesus Christ so that your sins may be forgiven; and you will receive the gift of the Holy Spirit.[121]

This first finding includes Luke's initial description of the Holy Spirit descending from heaven with the sound of violent rushing wind and divided tongues like fire resting upon each person present.

These recipients are identified by Luke as having received Holy Spirit baptism. Spirit baptism however was not meant to replace water baptism which continued to be an outward accompaniment and sign

---

[120] Acts 2:2-4
[121] Acts 2:38

of being inwardly baptized by the Spirit.[122] At this juncture repentance for forgiveness of sins and water baptism in the name of Jesus Christ is the only requirement for receiving the gift of Spirit baptism according to Luke's story.[123] Luke continues to pinpoint episodes of initiation into the Church through water baptism and Spirit baptism; however, the order or sequence of water baptism and Spirit baptism within each episode is not always the same.

The next case I will point out is the scenario where Luke records the first non-Jew being baptized in water in Acts 8, the Ethiopian eunuch. While Philip was spreading the good news of Jesus he encountered an Ethiopian eunuch. The eunuch was reading from the prophet Isaiah when Philip joined him and at the eunuch's request for clarification of the scripture Philip began to proclaim to the eunuch the good news about Jesus. After hearing this word, Philip baptized the eunuch in water and Luke simply states that the eunuch went on his way rejoicing. Luke does not state that the eunuch received Spirit baptism in v. 39. To this writer the fact that the Spirit of the Lord snatched Philip away implies that the Holy Spirit was in the midst of Philip and the Ethiopian eunuch. Since Philip had already received Spirit baptism it is only

---

[122] I. Howard Marshall, *The Acts of the Apostles: An Introduction and Commentary*, 194.

[123] John's baptism with water proclaimed a baptism of repentance for the forgiveness of sins (Luke 3). John's baptism was apocalyptic in nature looking toward the coming of the Anointed One, the Messiah. Holy Spirit baptism too is eschatological in that it sustains and empowers the Church in waiting for the return of Jesus to rule the kingdom of God on earth.

reasonable to accept that the eunuch received Spirit baptism too as a result of Philip's witness and the eunuch's keen inquiry into the good news about Jesus.

Luke does not portray that the Ethiopian eunuch relived the Pentecost experience communicated in Acts 2. There was no statement of violent wind, divided tongues, infilling with the Holy Spirit or speaking in another language. The second finding or point Luke made regarding baptism is quite unlike the first. Here (Acts 8) Luke presents a foreign Ethiopian eunuch being baptized in water after hearing the message about Jesus, the Messiah. The eunuch then went on his way rejoicing. Does this scene depict a legitimate initiation into the apocalyptic eschatological community, the Church? This writer affirms that it does when considering characterization techniques used by Luke within the framework of his ancient literary style.

In the story of the Ethiopian eunuch the text leaves an element of mystery regarding the character (the eunuch) and the audience is left to make the appropriate inference. This seems to fit into Gowler's description of indirect presentation:

> Indirect presentation . . . displays or exemplifies the qualities and traits of the characters, leaving the reader to make the appropriate inferences. Not only does the authority of the message vary, but the explicitness of the message itself varies.

> Any action, no matter how great or how small, no matter whether an act of commission, omission, or a contemplated act, may be of great importance as far as characterization is concerned.[124]

In order to appreciate Luke's characterization of the Ethiopian eunuch episode, Luke's ancient writing style must be understood.

Because I will be reviewing other appropriate texts I think it is important to evaluate Luke's writing style a bit more before leaving this discussion. Let us analyze the Ethiopian eunuch's environment in terms of his social class. His social class places him in a powerful higher echelon government position in his country. Luke depicts him reading from the prophet Isaiah. The environment is of great importance here as it sets the stage for the eunuch to act out his role and to be perceived positively by audiences.

Gowler explains that characterization can be supported by such things as primacy effect. "The primacy effect denotes the critical importance that initial information has upon the reader's process of perception."[125] Hence, Luke sets the stage when he initially describes the Ethiopian eunuch's government position and his reading of the scripture. It is readily believable and conceivable to readers in the end

---

[124] David B. Gowler, "Characterization in Luke: A Socio-Narratological Approach." *Biblical Theological Bulletin: A Journal of Bible and Theology* 19:1 (January 1989): 54-62.

[125] Ibid.

that the eunuch received Spirit baptism at some point and was initiated into the Church. Now that I have brought attention to Luke's literary style, I will examine another occasion when people are initiated into the Church community.

In this next case, Acts 10, Luke tells the story of Cornelius, a Gentile Roman government official, a God fearing man along with his family, a generous man who gives alms to people and a man who prays to God constantly. Here we see that Luke initially sets the stage as he describes Cornelius' social class and overall environment. Luke's characterization gives a persuasive edge to what his readers are about to hear in this scenario. While Peter was speaking of the good news about Jesus, the Messiah, the Holy Spirit fell on all who heard Peter's message including Cornelius, a Gentile (Acts 10:44). Cornelius was heard speaking in tongues by Peter and other circumcised believers who accompanied Peter (Acts 10:46) to Joppa. When explaining this incident to the Jerusalem Church leaders, Peter said the Holy Spirit fell on them (Gentiles) just as it had on those at the beginning meaning at the Pentecost celebration (Acts 11:15).

This finding shows that Cornelius was initiated into the Church community the same as the Jews at the Pentecost experience (Acts 11:16). [126] In this writer's view Luke-Acts establishes a prerequisite for

---

[126] In Acts 2:1-4 Luke omits making the statement that the Jewish audience was baptized in water. However, it is understood that they were baptized in water and received the gift of the Holy Spirit (Spirit baptism). The characters in Acts

being initiated into the Church: hearing the message of Jesus the Christ, repentance, water baptism and Spirit baptism (Acts 2:38). In key texts referred to previously Luke does not establish a precise order or sequence in which water baptism and Spirit baptism must occur. Luke does however illustrate in key text evaluated previously that candidates for initiation into the Church first hear the spoken word about Jesus, the Messiah, (Acts 1:5; 2:37, 41; 8:12, 35; 10:44; 19:4-5) and then they respond thereto. This is the model or pattern identified by Luke as being necessary to gain entrance into the apocalyptic eschatological community (the Church) awaiting the return of Jesus to reign over the kingdom of God.

Conclusion

In this chapter I have examined the relationship between water baptism and Spirit baptism, compared Pentecostal and Charismatic church beliefs and practices regarding water and Spirit baptism and identified Luke's prerequisite for being initiated into the Church. Now I will revisit my initial inquiry into this study. What are the origins or roots of water baptism? This study clearly shows that water baptism practiced in the contemporary Christian Church draws its roots or origins directly from beliefs and practices of ancient Jews. Focus on the

---

2:1-4 were following Jesus instructions as they were all assembled together on one accord when the Holy Spirit arrived at the Pentecost celebration.

Luke-Acts account of water baptism has been the source for drawing some culmination concerning water baptism on the basis of antecedents. It was during the Jewish Pentecost festival (ca. 33 C.E.) that the Church began and thousands were initiated into the Church through water baptism (Acts 2:41) and Spirit baptism (Acts 1:5; 2:1-5).[127]

This Jewish Pentecost celebration signaled the commencement of Spirit baptism. Once believers had been initiated into the Church community Luke explains that all were together and had all things in common (Acts 2:44). This principle continues in the contemporary Christian Church. Water baptism was practiced amidst various other water rituals in Judaism long before the institution of the Church through Priestly purification water rites, Qumran water rites, Pharisaic water rites, proselyte water baptism and John's water baptism for instance. When the Church was born it simply mimicked the accepted religious practice of water baptism. In Luke-Acts it appears that this new situation of the Church community worked well in the early stages.

The Church grew from a predominantly Jewish assembly in the beginning to a more Gentile community as time passed. It appears that the latter group eventually gave rise to Gentiles staking claim on the whole of the Christian Church initiation process with little or no

---

[127] The methodology for accomplishing water baptism in ancient Jewish practices was administered through immersion much like it is in the many Christian churches today.

consideration of origins of water baptism. Most Christians today rarely mention the fact that the practice of water baptism is an offspring of Judaism. Thus, an automatic wedge between Christianity and Judaism becomes apparent. When the Church was born there was no immediate divide between Christianity and Judaism.[128] In a sense Christianity could be simply seen as a new sect of Judaism. Jewish Jesus followers continued to act in a celebratory manner bringing offerings to God.

My study on the origin of water baptism reveals that Jewish water rites are an antecedent of baptism. Why should Christians today acknowledge this finding? How would it improve their understanding of the Bible, OT and NT? In this writer's view it would be a powerful Bible study tool. Contemporary Christians would be better informed if they had a working knowledge of how water baptism came about. This understanding could be integrated with the understanding of Spirit baptism and a clearer picture of the Pentecostal experience (e.g., water and Spirit baptism) could evolve. Hence, Christians and Jews could once again align with the understanding of the richness of their legacy surrounding the Pentecostal experience with a fuller awareness of what may be seen as a vicarious legacy between contemporary Christians and Jews.

---

[128] The term "Christianity" used here refers to the "Jesus followers." At the inception of the Church the term "Christianity" was not used. The more appropriate terminology, "Jesus followers," refers to those Jews who heard and accepted the message of Jesus, the Messiah, and were initiated into the Church community.

Today Judaism membership is small in number compared to Christianity. Yet, when the Church was formulated about two thousand years ago these two groups began to share a major feast, Pentecost. This feast day is still celebrated in Judaism and Christianity. I suggest that Christians could begin to share in the Jewish Passover celebration in anticipation of the Pentecost feast day. Both groups could then celebrate Pentecost in a manner suitable to each. Thus, dialogue between Christians and Jews could become a common occurrence.

The problem for this writer on the subject of origin of water baptism has been motivated not because it is used as part of the initiation process in most all contemporary Christian churches in the world but because the teachings on the initiation process are flawed. It is this writer's view that most of Christendom today seems to consider the initiation process into the church as being developed by today's mostly Gentile church. This is not so. We could simply continue teaching as usual and leave flawed and unclear thinking in place. Would this change the physical initiation practice itself? No. Could the Church today improve on its teaching on the subject by acknowledging that water baptism is an antecedent of the Jews? Yes. For instance, when teaching from Acts 2 they could simply point out that water baptism was a Jewish antecedent.

What remains to be done in the contemporary Christian churches today? This answer could only be that more teaching to open up Bible class participation and study is needed. Discontinuing embedded traditional Bible teaching is also needed. The lack of teaching on the subject of water baptism in the Church today causes a mammoth misunderstanding of Bible hermeneutics. This study on origins of water baptism is open-ended as new minds come forth teaching from the OT and NT exegetically.

Bibliography

Akli, Lawrence Perry. *The Pauline Concept of Baptism and New Life in Christ: The Dynamics of Christian Life According to St. Paul*. Romae: N. Domenici-Pecheux, 1992.

Aland, Kurt. *Did the Early Church Baptize Infants?* Philadelphia: The Westminister Press, 1963.

_____. *Synopsis of the Four Gospels RSV*. New York: American Bible Society, 1985.

Allen, Ronald J. "The Story of the Church According to 'Luke' - The Acts of the Apostles" in *Chalice Introduction to the New Testament,* ed. D. Smith. St. Louis: Chalice Press, 2004.

_____. "The Story of Jesus According to 'Luke' - The Gospel of Luke" in *Chalice Introduction to the New Testament,* ed. Dennis Smith. St. Louis: Chalice Press, 2004.

Allen, Ronald J. and Clark M. Williamson. *Preaching the Gospels Without Blaming the Jews - A Lectionary Commentary.* Louisville: Westminster John Knox Press, 2004.

Allison, Dale C., Jr. "The Baptism of Jesus and a New Dead Sea Scroll." *Biblical Archaeology Review* 18 (March/April 1992): 58-60.

Aune, David E. *The New Testament in Its Literary Environment.* ed. by Wayne E. Meeks. Philadelphia: The Westminister Press, 1987.

Barth, Karl. *Church Dogmatics IV.4 The Doctrine of Reconciliation.*, eds. G.W. Bromiley, T.F. Torrance. London: T&T Clark International A Continuum, 1969.

Beasley-Murray, G. R. *Baptism in the New Testament.* London: MacMillan & Co Ltd, 1962.

Blomberg, Craig L. "The Law In Luke-Acts," *Journal for the Study of the New Testament* 22 (1984): 53-80.

Brawley, Robert L. *Luke-Acts and the Jews – Conflict, Apology, and Conciliation*. Society of Biblical Literature Monograph Series No. 33. Atlanta: Scholars Press, 1987.

Buse, S.E. "Baptism in the Acts of the Apostles." *In Christian Baptism: A Fresh Attempt to Understand the Tire in Terms of Scripture, History and Theology*, ed. A. Gilmore, intro. E.A. Payne Chicago: Judson Press, 1959.

Campbell, Alexander. *Christian Baptism With Its Antecedents and Consequents,* ed. Nashville: Gospel Advocate Co., 1951.

Cullmann, Oscar. *Studies in Biblical Theology: Baptism in the New Testament*, J.K.S. Reid, trans. London: SCM Press LTD, 1950.

Cullpepper, R. Alan. "The Gospel of Luke" in *The New Interpreter's Bible*. Nashville: Abingdon Press, 1995.

Dale James W. *Judaic Baptism BAΠTIZΩ: An Inquiry Into the Meaning of the Word As Determined By the Usage of Jewish and Patristic Writers*. Wauconda: Bolchazy-Carducci Publishers: P&RCo.: Loewe Belfort Projects, Inc., 1991.

Eck, Diana L. *Encountering God: A Spiritual Journey from Bozeman to Banaras.* Boston: Beacon Press, 1993.

Eliade, Mircea. *Patterns in Comparative Religion*, trans. R. Sheed. New York: Sheed & Ward, 1958.

Finkelstein, Louis. "The Institution of Baptism for Proselytes." *Journal of Biblical Literature* LII (1933): 203-210.

Fitzmyer, Joseph A. "The Gospel According to Luke" (I-IX) in *The Anchor Bible* 28. Garden City: Doubleday & Company, Inc., 1981.

_____. "The Gospel According to Luke" (X-XXIV) in *The Anchor Bible* 28A. New York: Doubleday, 1985.

Gavin, F. *Jewish Antecedents of the Christian Sacraments.* London: Society for Promoting Christian Knowledge, 1928.

Gilmore, Alec. "Jewish Antecedents" in *Christian Baptism - A Fresh Attempt to Understand the Rite in terms of Scripture, History and Theology,* ed. A. Gilmore. Chicago: Judson Press, 1959.

Gowler, David B. "Characterization in Luke: A Socio-Narratological Approach." *Biblical Theological Bulletin - A Journel of Bible and Theology* 19:1 (January 1989): 54-62.

Guy, Laurie. *Introducing Early Christianity: A Topical Survey of Its Life, Belief And Practices.* Downers Grove: InterVarsity Press, 2004.

Hyatt, J. Philip. "The Origin and Meaning of Christian Baptism." *Encounter* 21:1 (Winter 1960): 255-268.

Jeremias, Joachim. *The Origins of Infant Baptism - A Further Study in Reply to Kurt Aland.* Eugene: Wipf & Stock Publishers, 2004.

Jervell, Jacob. *The Unknown Paul:Essays on Luke-Acts and Early Christian History* Minneapolis: Augsburg Publishing House, 1984.

Johnson, Maxwell. *The Rites of Christian Initiation: Their Evolution and Interpretation* Collegeville: The Liturgical Press, 1999.

Kavanagh, Aidan. *The Shape of Baptism: The Rite of Christian Initiation.* Collegeville: The Liturgical Press, 1978.

Lathrop, Gordon W. "Baptism in the New Testament and its Cultural Settings" in *LWF 3 Worship and Culture in Dialogue*, ed. S. Anita Stauffer. Geneva: The Lutheran World Federation, 1994.

La Sor, William Sanford. Discovering What Jewish Miqva'ot Can Tell Us About Christian Baptism." *Biblical Archaeology Review* 1 (January/February 1987): 52-59.

Lumpkin, William L. *A History of Immersion*, eds. E.A. Castelli, H. Taussig. Nashville: Broadman Press, 1962.

Mack, Burton L. *Reimagining Christian Origins: A Colloquium Honoring Burton L. Mack*. Valley Forge: Trinity Press International, 1996.

Marshall, I. Howard. *The Acts of the Apostles: An Introduction and Commentary*. Leicester: Inter-Varsity Press, Wm. B. Eerdmans Publishing Company, 1980.

Martinez, F. Garcia and Julio Trebolle Barrera. *The People of the Dead Sea Scrolls: Their Writings, Beliefs and Practices*. trans. Wilfred G.E. Watson, Leiden: Brill, 1995.

Meeks, Wayne A. gen. ed. et al. *New Harper Collins Study Bible, NRSV*. New York: Harper Collins Publishers, 1993.

Mell, Glen. *Jewish Proselyte Baptism and its Relation to Christian Baptism.* Thesis (M.A.) Indianapolis: Butler University, 1938.

Murphy, Catherine M. *John the Baptist: Prophet of Purity for a New Age.* Collegeville: Liturgical Press, 2003.

Neusner, Jacob. *The Judaic Law of Baptism: Tractate Miqvaot in the Mishnah and the Tosefta: A Form-Analytical Translation and Commentary and a Legal and Religious History.* Atlanta: Scholars Press, 1995.

_____. *Judaism in the Beginning of Christianity.* Philadelphia: Fortress Press, 1984.

Nolland, John. "Luke 1:1-9:20" in *Word Biblical Commentary* Vol 35A, eds. B. Metzger et al. Columbia: Nelson Reference & Electronic (div. of Thomas Nelson Publishers), 1989.

_____. "Luke 9:21-18:34" in *Word Biblical Commentary* Vol 35B, eds. B. Metzger et al. Columbia: Nelson Reference & Electronic (div. of Thomas Nelson Publishers), 1993.

_____. "Luke 18:35-24:53" in *Word Biblical Commentary* Vol 35C, eds. B. Metzger et al. Columbia: Nelson Reference & Electronic (div. of Thomas Nelson Publishers), 1993.

Organizational Manual *2004 Minute Book*. Indianapolis: Pentecostal Assemblies of the World, Inc., 2005.

Osborne, Kenan B. *The Christian Sacraments of Initiation: Baptism, Confirmation, Eucharist*. New York: Paulist Press, 1987.

Peagnant, Russell. *Engaging the New Testament: An Interdisciplinary Introduction*. Minneapolis: Fortress Press, 1995.

Pervo, Richard I. *Luke's Story of Paul* Minneapolis: Fortress Press, 1990.

Porter, Stanley E. *Baptism, the New Testament and the Church*, eds. St. Porter, A. Cross, Sheffield: Sheffield Academic Press, 1999.

Powell, Mark Allan. *What Are They Saying About Luke?* New York: Paulist Press, 1989.

_____. *Dimensions of Baptism Biblical and Theological Studies*, eds. St. Porter, A. Cross. London: Sheffield Academic Press, 2002.

Pryke, John. "The Sacraments of Holy Baptism and Holy Communion In the Light of The Ritual Washings and Sacred Meals at Qumran." *Revue De Qumran* 17 (October 1964): 543-552.

Pusey, Karen and John Hunt. "Jewish Proselyte Baptism." *The Expository Times* 95:1 (October 1983): 141-145.

Ricks, Stephen D. "Miqvaot: Ritual Immersion Baths in Second Temple (Intertestamental) Jewish History." *BYU Studies* 36 3 (1996-1997): 277-286.

Schnackenburg, Rudolf. *Baptism in the Thought of St. Paul: A Study in Pauline Theology,* trans. by G.R. Beasley-Murray. Oxford: Basil Blackwell, 1964.

Skarsaune, Oskar. *In the Shadow of the Temple: Jewish Influences on Early Christianity.* Downers Grove: InterVarsity Press, 2002.

Smith, Derwood. "Jewish Proselyte Baptism and the Baptism of John." *Restoration Quarterly* 25:1 (first quarter 1982): 13-32.

Smith, Dennis E., ed. *Chalice Introduction to the New Testament.* St. Louis: Chalice Press, 2004.

Stauffer, S. Anita, ed. *Worship and Culture in Dialogue*. Geneva: Lutheran World Federation, 1994.

Talbert, Charles H. *Reading Luke-Acts In Its Mediterranean Milieu*. Leiden: Brill, 2003.

Tan, Simon G.H. "Reassessing Believer's Baptism in Pentecostal Theology and Practice." *Asian Journal of Pentecostal Studies* 6:2 (2003): 219-234.

Tannehill, Robert C. *The Narrative Unity of Luke-Acts: A Literary Interpretation, Vol. 1: The Gospel according to Luke*. Philadelphia: Fortress Press, 1986.

_____. *The Narrative Unity of Luke-Acts: A Literary Interpretation, Vol. 2: The Acts of the Apostles*. Minneapolis: Fortress Press, 1990.

Torrance, T.F. "The Origins of Baptism." *Scottish Journal of Theology* 11 (March 1958): 158-71.

Turner, Max. "The Work of the Holy Spirit in Luke-Acts." *Word & World* 23 (2003): 146-153.

Wedderburn, A.J.M. *Baptism and Resurrection: Studies in Pauline Theology Against Its Graeco-Roman Background.* Tübingen: J.C.B. Mohr (Paul Siebeck), 1987.

Williamson, Clark M. *The Nature of the Church 4 - Baptism: Embodiment of the Gospel - Disciples Baptismal Theology.* St. Louis: Christian Board of Publication, 1987.

Wilson, Marvin R. *Our Father Abraham: Jewish Roots of the Christian Faith.* Grand Rapids: William B. Eerdmans Publishing Co. and Dayton: Center for Judaic-Christian Studies, 1989.

Yun, Koo Dong. "Water Baptism and Spirit Baptism: Pentecostals and Lutherans in Dialogue." Ecumenic and Ecumenical Perspectives. *Dialog: A Journal of Theology* 43 (Winter 2004): 344-350.

Zeitlin, Solomon. "The Halaka In The Gospels And Its Relation To The Jewish Law at The Time Of Jesus." *Hebrew Union College Annual* 1.01 (2006): 357-373.

Printed in the United States
By Bookmasters